STANDARD GRADE HISTORY

Co-operation and Conflict: International Relations

1890-1930

J A Harkness, H McMillan and D Moore

Hodder & Stoughton
LONDON SYDNEY AUCKLAND

Acknowledgements

The Publishers would like to thank the following for permission to reproduce material in this volume:
Basil Blackwell for the extract from *The First World War* by Barry Bates; Blackie And Son Ltd for the extracts from *The First World War* by L F Hobley (1971); Malcolm Brown for the extracts from *Christmas Truce* by Brown and Seaton (1984); Collins/Angus & Robertson for the extract from *Behind the Lines: One Woman's War* by A J P Taylor (1961); Heinemann Ltd for the extracts from *Daily Mail* dated April 2nd 1915; Faber and Faber Ltd for the extracts from *Old Soldiers Never Die* by Frank Richards; Hamish Hamilton for the extract from *The Origins of the Second World War* by A J P Taylor (1961); Heineman Ltd for the extracts from *War Beyond Britain* by Fiona Reynoldson and *The Drift to War* by Stone; HMSO for the extracts from *Documents on the origins of the war 1898-1914* by G P Gooch and H W Temperley (1930); Michael Joseph Ltd for the extracts from *Voices and Images of the Great War* by Lyn Macdonald © Lyn Macdonald 1988; Longman Group Ltd for the extracts from *Europe 1880-1945* by J M Roberts (1967), *The League and the U.N.O.* by Gibbons and Morican, and *The Weimar Republic* by J W Hiden (1984); Macmillan Publishers Ltd for the extract from *Useful Toil* ed. J Burnett; Macmillan Publishing Company (USA) for the extracts from *The Genesis of War* by H H Asquith (Cassell, 1923), *Memoirs and Reflections, Volume 2* by H H Asquith (Cassell, 1928) and *The German High Seas* by Admiral Reinhard Scheer (Cassell, 1920); Methuen & Co. for the extracts from *Britain Between the Wars* by C L Mowat; Mirror Group Newspapers Ltd for the extracts from *The Daily Record* dated May 8th 1917; extracts from *Speeches and Documents in American History* by Robert Birley (1942) and *Twentieth Century Britain* (2nd Edition) by W Robson (1983) reproduced by permission of Oxford University Press; extracts from *White Heat* by John Terraine reprinted by permission of the Peters Fraser & Dunlop Group Ltd; *'In Flanders fields'* by John McCrae, reproduced by permission of Punch (1915); *'Suicide in the Trenches'* by Siegfried Sassoon reproduced by permission of George Sassoon; Secker and Warburg for the extract from *The Twelve Days* by George Malcolm Thomson (1964); Sheil Land Associates Ltd for the extracts from *Voices 1870-1914* © Peter Vansittart; the extract from *Turn of the century* by Hoare reproduced by permission of Simon & Schuster Young Books, Hemel Hempstead, UK; Thames & Hudson Ltd for the extracts from *From Sarajevo to Potsdam* by A J P Taylor; Stanley Thornes for the extract from *Europe in Conflict – A History of Europe 1870-1970* by A Jamieson; the Trustees of the Imperial War Museum for the extracts from *With a Machine Gun to Cambrai* by G Coppard; A P Watt Ltd, on behalf of the Trustees of the Robert Graves Copyright Trust for the extracts from *Goodbye To All That* by R Graves (1929).
Every effort has been made to trace and acknowledge ownership of copyright. The publishers will be glad to make suitable arrangements with any copyright holders whom it has not been possible to contact.

The publishers would like to thank the following for permission to reproduce copyright illustrations:
Author p1; Bild Archiv der Osterreichischen Nationalbibliothik, Wien p24 right, 25 left; David Low-Evening Standard/Centre for the Study of Cartoons and Caricature, University of Kent at Canterbury/Solo Syndication p70 bottom; Edimedia p7 top, 20; Illustrated London News Picture Library p26 left; Imperial War Museum cover, p14,17 top, 23 top right, 30,33 both, 34 top, 38 left, 39 left, 42, 43 left both, 44,47 both, 52,53,55; Mansell Collection p18 right, 21,22 bottom right and top, 23 top left, 24 top, 27,28; Mary Evans Picture Library p23 bottom right; Popperfoto p3,9,15,17 bottom; Reproduced by permission of Punch p2,4 top, 5,12 both, 16,25 right, 29,31,34 bottom, 49,51,60,62,75; The Bettmann Archive/Hulton Picture Company p72; The Hulton Picture Company p4 bottom, 6,11,26 right, 32,38 right, 39 right, 43 right, 48,54 left, 63,66,69 top, 73 right; The Labour Party p67 both; Ullstein Bilderdienst p35,36,64 both, 65; Weimar Archive p22 bottom left.

Also in the series:
International Relations 1930-60 ISBN 0 340 54211 X
Robert Doig

Changing Life in Scotland and Britain 1750-1850 ISBN 0 340 53282 3
Craig Madden

Scotland and Britain 1830-1980 ISBN 0 340 54212 8
S A S Chalmers and Larry Cheyne

People and Power: Germany 1918-39 ISBN 0 340 54213 6
Ian Matheson

British Library Cataloguing in Publication Data
Harkness, James A.
Co-operation and conflict: international relations 1890-1930. – (Standard grade history)
I. Title II. McMillan, Hugh III. Moore, David
IV. Series
940.2

ISBN 0 340 54214 4

First published 1991. Second impression 1992

Typeset by Litho Link Limited, Welshpool, Powys, Wales
Printed in Great Britain for the educational publishing division of Hodder & Stoughton Ltd, Mill Road, Dunton Green, Sevenoaks, Kent by M & A Thomson Litho Ltd, East Kilbride, Scotland.

Contents

SERIES PREFACE

The books in this series are designed to present major historical themes, change, co-operation and conflict, people and power. Key ideas in British, European and World history derived from these themes provide the basis for the organisation of content. The books make use of different types of evidence – primary and secondary, written, statistical and pictorial. Users of the books are guided towards their own understanding of history, based on their individual abilities and interests, as each section (chapter) progresses from simpler statements of ideas and issues to a consideration and analysis of more detailed and complex evidence.

It is the hope of the authors that the books in the series will increase understanding of the chosen themes as well as enthusiasm for investigating people, actions and events in history. Those who use the books will be encouraged to decide for themselves about the evidence they contain and to have their own views of the past.

Graeme Coy.

1 WE ARE THE DEAD

A The grave of VJ Strudwick of The Rifle Brigade, who died on 14 January 1916 at Ypres, aged 15.

Amongst the graves where Strudwick was buried, an Army Surgeon called John McCrae noticed poppies growing and he wrote these words.

B In Flanders fields the poppies blow
Between the crosses, row on row
That mark our place; and in the sky
The larks still bravely singing, fly
Scarce heard amid the groans below.
We are the Dead. Short days ago
We lived, felt dawn, saw sunset glow,
Loved and were loved, and now we lie
In Flanders fields.

John McCrae, written during the 2nd Battle of Ypres (1915)

CO-OPERATION AND CONFLICT

In 1900 VJ Strudwick was born in England. When Strudwick was young, Europe was united in a way which has not been matched since (according to the historian A J P Taylor).

C In 1914 Europe was a single civilized community. A man could travel across the whole continent without a passport until he reached Russia or the Turkish Empire.

AJP Taylor – From Sarajevo to Potsdam

When Strudwick was at his first lessons, he might have heard about the German Emperor, *Kaiser Wilhelm II*. Germany already had a large army and, from the year 1900 onwards, Wilhelm began to build a large navy. Germany's European neighbours were worried by the Kaiser's actions and formed alliances to protect themselves from Germany.

In August 1914 Britain went to war and VJ Strudwick broke the law, by joining the army. He trained as a soldier but, by January 1916, he lay dead in a field in Flanders (Belgium) – a victim of the Great War.

For four long years the war dragged on. When it finished in November 1918, the casualty lists were truly horrific.

D Killed during the First World War

Country	Killed
Great Britain	761,213
France	1,385,000
Russia	1,700,000 (estimate)
Germany	2,000,000
Austria–Hungary	1,100,000

THE HISTORICAL JIGSAW

International Relations 1890–1930

Studying this period in history is like doing a jigsaw. Before we can see the whole picture, all the pieces have to be fitted together. The 'pieces' in history are called *evidence* and, in writing this book, we have used evidence to describe events, to explain why certain things happened, and to explain why people acted as they did. Through the words and images of the people who lived at the time, we hope to bring the story to life.

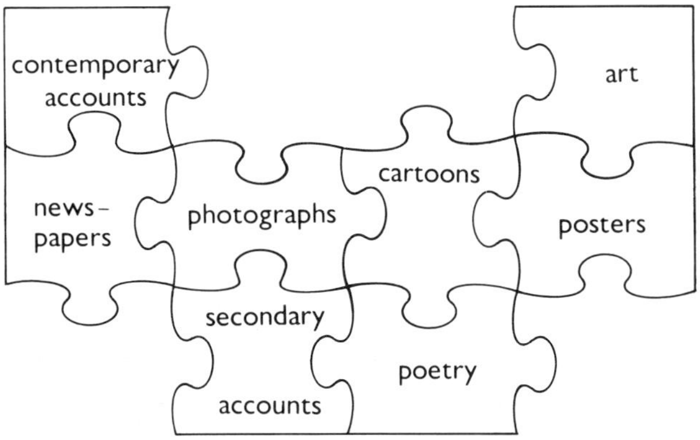

E The Jigsaw of Evidence.

In a book, though, it is possible to choose only a few examples from the sources of information illustrated above. We have therefore been able to choose only sources which can be printed.

Example 1 – Cartoons

The following cartoon was published a few years before VJ Strudwick was born. It shows the effects of the Kaiser's actions on other European leaders. Look carefully at the cartoon. In the rowing boat you can see the Kaiser standing on the seat rocking the boat. In the stern are the other European leaders (notice the crowns). They are holding on and warning the Kaiser that his actions are going to get them all into trouble.

[Reproduced by permission of the Proprietors of 'Punch.'

L'ENFANT TERRIBLE!

CHORUS IN THE STERN. "DON'T GO ON LIKE THAT—OR YOU'LL UPSET US ALL!"

F This British cartoon shows how the Kaiser was causing instability in Europe before 1914.

Cartoons like this are useful because they can illustrate complicated actions in a simple way. In this case, however, the cartoonist is British so we must remember that his views are one-sided (or biased).

Example 2 – Poetry

G Suicide in the Trenches

I knew a simple soldier boy
Who grinned at life in empty joy,
Slept soundly through the lonesome dark,
and whistled early with the lark.

In winter trenches, cowed and glum,
With crumps and lice and lack of rum,
He put a bullet through his brain.
No-one spoke of him again.

You smug-faced crowds with kindling eye
Who cheer when soldier lads march by,
Sneak home and pray you'll never know
The hell where youth and laughter go.

Siegfried Sassoon (1917)

From war poetry we can learn about the experience of war and also about the attitudes of some of those who fought.

Example 3 – Photographs

H Trench conditions.

There is a wealth of photographic evidence from this period – and we have made great use of it. Most photographs simply record scenes or people, but historians need to be aware that some have been specially posed. Where these are deliberately used to affect our feelings, they are a form of propaganda. (For example, see pages 6, 35 and 66.)

Example 4 – Contemporary Accounts

This account of an incident in the trenches was written by Frank Richards in a book called *Old Soldiers Never Die*

I We took turns in one part of the trench bailing out water with a bucket. One morning, a man named Davies had his thumb shot off whilst bailing. The next man deliberately invited a bullet through his hands by exposing them a little longer than necessary – but the bucket got riddled instead.

There are many examples of old soldiers who wrote about their experiences. These accounts are valuable to us since the soldiers describe events in which they took part.

Missing Evidence

Listed above are only a few examples of the kinds of evidence we have been able to use to build up a picture of the events of the years between 1890 and 1930. We could not use all the evidence in a book. Instead, you should try to make use of some of the following types of source in your study of this period. In that way you will learn a lot more and the experience will be more enjoyable.

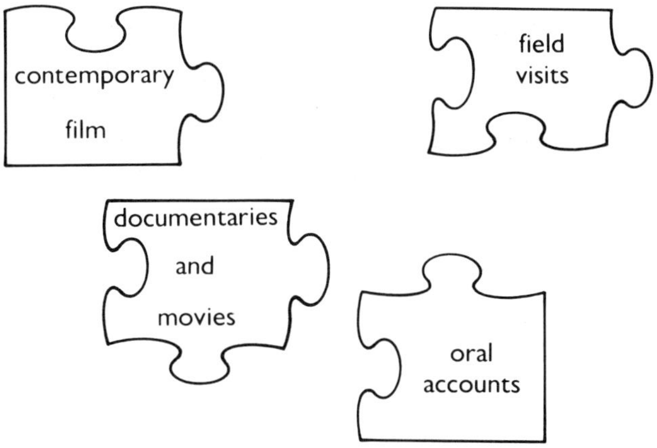

J Evidence we could not use.

The period 1890–1930 was full of excitement and drama. In these years the old world of the nineteenth century disappeared for ever and a new era began. America became a major power, Britain's importance declined and the horrors of war led people to try to settle future quarrels in other ways. Through the words and images of those who lived in the time, this book tries to capture the excitement of the period.

?

1. Explain why using evidence is so important in History.
2. In what ways are contemporary sources like sources F, G, H and I useful for historians?
3. **Class Discussion**: What features of a source are important in deciding whether or not it is valuable to a historian carrying out a particular study?

2 THE KAISER'S GERMANY

[Reproduced by permission of the Proprietors of 'Punch.'

DROPPING THE PILOT.

Punch's most famous political cartoon. William II and Bismarck part company. Both of them, strangely enough, liked this representation.

A Bismarck steps down from the ship *Germany* leaving Kaiser Wilhelm in sole charge – a Punch cartoon from 1890.

In 1890 there was a change in the leadership of Germany. Bismarck, who had been Chancellor for many years, was dropped from the government. For twenty years he had kept Germany at peace. He was always careful in dealing with other world leaders and encouraged them not to fear Germany. Bismarck had controlled German affairs and even told the Kaiser what to do! But, in 1888, Wilhelm II became Kaiser and he was not willing to listen to Bismarck.

B There is only one master in Germany and I am he.

Kaiser Wilhelm II (1888)

Kaiser Wilhelm was not like Bismarck. He was rude, impulsive and always wanted things done his way. He also had such a terrible temper that even members of the German government thought he might be mad.

Kaiser Wilhelm's strange behaviour meant that he was not trusted by politicians. But then the Kaiser did not trust them either. 'My trust,' he said, 'is placed in the army'. When the military offered advice, the Kaiser listened. The advice they gave alarmed those who wanted peace for the Kaiser was reminded that wars had brought Germany glory, wealth and territory. The Kaiser claimed that building up the army showed his peaceful intentions. He said:

C He who wishes for peace, let him prepare for war.

Kaiser Wilhelm II (1890)

D The Kaiser in uniform – This was his favourite form of dress. His war helmet features a dove – usually a symbol of peace.

E This table shows the number of soldiers the Great Powers had.

	1880	1914
Germany	1,300,000	5,000,000
France	740,000	4,000,000
Russia	400,000	1,200,000
Austria–Hungary	770,000	800,000
Britain	400,000	700,000

After 1872 Germany was the strongest country in Europe. Bismarck always tried to tell neighbouring countries that Germany had everything she wanted. The Kaiser however was not satisfied with what Germany had in 1890. He admired the British Empire and wanted colonies for Germany. 'Germany must have its place in the sun', he announced. However, Germany had entered the race for colonies too late as the world was now divided up amongst the other Great Powers. 'How would Germany obtain colonies?' people asked. 'The world belongs to the strong', came the reply.

The Kaiser's huge army meant that any threat he made was taken seriously. Some Germans thought that the other Great Powers took the Kaiser too seriously.

F He only wanted to impress them so that they'd think that he was another Napoleon or Frederick the Great.

Prince von Bülow (German Chancellor 1900-1909)

The Kaiser believed Germany to be so strong that she need fear no one. Bismarck, a wiser man, did not have the same view. Germany must prevent countries forming alliances against her, especially France, Britain and Russia.

G These three would make an Alliance against Germany more dangerous than any other she might face.

Otto von Bismarck (1885)

However, France, Britain and Russia hated each other so much that, in 1890, such an alliance was impossible. Even so, a growing fear of Germany very soon placed them all in the same boat.

[Reproduced by permission of the Proprietors of 'Punch.'

L'ENFANT TERRIBLE!

CHORUS IN THE STERN. "DON'T GO ON LIKE THAT—OR YOU'LL UPSET US ALL!"

H The Kaiser's antics alarmed other European leaders.

?

1. What do sources A and H tell us about the power of the Kaiser?
2. According to sources, B, C, D and E, why might a rival country fear Germany more after 1890?
3. (a) What alliance of countries did Bismarck fear most?
   (b) Why was such an alliance unlikely in 1890?
4. **Discussion**: Work in pairs and use sources B, C, E, F, and the text to help you.

   The Kaiser said, 'I want . . .'
   (a) Write down three possible endings to this sentence.
   (b) Write down an explanation for each completed statement.
   Discuss your answers.

QUARRELSOME NEIGHBOURS

France Quarrels with Germany

France was the only great power which seemed determined on war with Germany. French hostility was due to the events of 1871. In that year, France – the most powerful nation in the world – was defeated and humiliated by Germany.

I I can feel already the coming of that immense revenge . . . Oh! then France will be a power to reckon with. We will see her at a single stroke, resume possession of Alsace-Lorraine.

Victor Hugo speaking to the French parliament (1872)

Defeat cost the French people more than hurt pride. France was forced to pay Germany huge sums in reparations and give up the valuable border lands of Alsace-Lorraine.

K The following tables show the strength of France compared with the other Great Powers.

(a) Steel produced each year in millions of tonnes

	1890	**1900**	**1910**
Britain	3.6	5.0	6.5
France	0.7	1.6	3.4
Germany	2.2	6.6	13.7
Russia	0.4	2.2	3.5
Italy	0.1	0.1	0.7

(b) Population increases (in millions)

	1890	**1900**	**1910**
Britain	40	47.0	51.4
France	40	40.7	41.5
Germany	44.2	50.6	58.5
Russia	115	131.7	153.8

From JM Roberts (1967) – Europe 1880–1945

While French people longed for the opportunity to fight a war of revenge against Germany, the growing strength of her rival made it unlikely that France could ever defeat Germany on her own.

J The birth of the German Empire is announced from the Hall of Mirrors, Versailles.

L French children stand beside an 1871 war memorial and gaze over the lost lands of Alsace-Lorraine.

Clearly, France needed an ally but, in 1890, she had more enemies than friends.

● *Britain and France: Imperial Rivals*

During the nineteenth century, the Great Powers had divided up the world amongst themselves, with Britain receiving the lion's share. The 'Scramble for Africa', especially, caused a great deal of ill feeling.

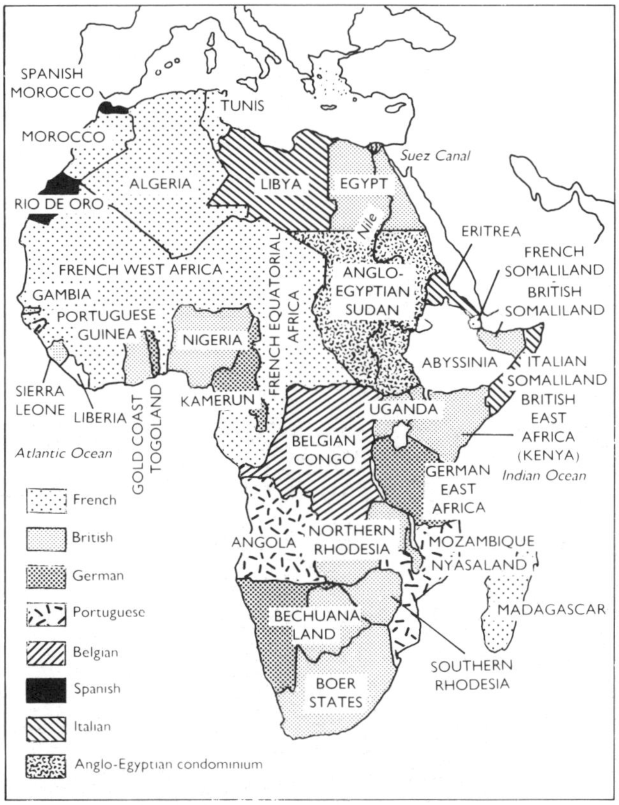

M In the scramble for Africa, France came second. Britain took the most valuable areas.

N We were constantly having friction over Africa. It was not very comfortable, even so far as Germany was concerned, but as regards France and Russia, the situation was very much worse.

Sir Edward Grey (1911) – British Foreign Minister

France and Britain became such bitter rivals over colonies that war between them seemed likely. In 1898 there was a crisis over the small town of *Fashoda* in the Sudan. Ownership of the town was claimed by both Britain and France. So strong was French feeling against Britain that even Alsace-Lorraine became, for the moment, of secondary importance.

O Our hatred of Germany can be wiped out but England is the enemy of yesterday, tomorrow and forever.

French journalist (1898)

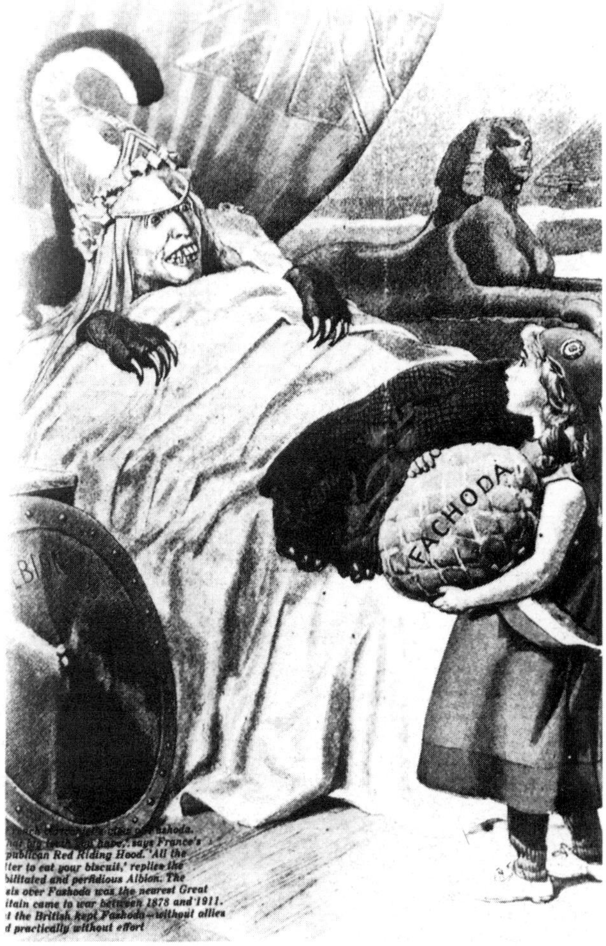

P French cartoon on the Fashoda Crisis.

Britain and France: Enemies of Russia

Britain and Russia were not on good terms in 1890. Russian ambition in the Balkans was seen as a threat to Britain's trade route through the Suez Canal. Furthermore, it was believed that Russia wanted to rule India, one of the most valuable parts of the British Empire.

Like Britain, France was also a traditional enemy of Russia. The two countries had very different systems of government, with the leader of France elected by the people while the leader of Russia was chosen by God. Bismarck's fear that France, Britain and Russia might unite against Germany therefore seemed very unlikely at that time.

Britain Quarrels with Germany

In 1899, however, Britain went to war with two tiny South African Boer Republics. It took the British army three years to defeat an army of farmers. British tactics (such as her use of concentration camps for prisoners) were widely condemned, both in Britain and in other countries

The Kaiser openly supported the Boers and twice suggested an alliance of the other Great Powers against Britain. However, such an alliance was not formed, mainly because of the strength of the Royal Navy. The Boer War was therefore of great importance for several reasons. Firstly, Britain's isolation was now seen as a weakness rather than an advantage. Furthermore, the importance of a strong navy was more greatly appreciated in both Britain and Germany. The latter, learning a lesson from the war, now argued more strongly for a high seas fleet of her own.

In 1898 some leading British politicians had suggested an alliance between Britain and Germany. The Kaiser's actions during the Boer War ended these discussions. Increasingly, Germany was seen by Britain as a threat, rather than as a friend. But would fear of Germany become strong enough to force Britain, France and Russia to forget their differences?

Q A British cartoon showing a British soldier kicking a pregnant South African woman.

?

1. Using sources I, J and L, explain why France was determined to go to war with Germany.
2. From your study of the tables in source K, why was it becoming less likely that France would defeat Germany on its own?
3. According to sources, M, N, O, P, and the text, what prevented Britain, France and Russia from becoming friends?
4. Why might Bismarck have thought the Kaiser's intervention in the Boer War unwise?

3

TWO ARMED CAMPS

● *The Triple Alliance*

In 1871 France was defeated by Germany. Bismarck, then Chancellor of Germany, did not think that peace would last but he knew that France was too weak to fight Germany on her own. To maintain peace he formed alliances to keep France without friends. The most important of these was signed in 1882 when Germany, together with Italy and Austria-Hungary, formed a grouping called the Triple Alliance (see map).

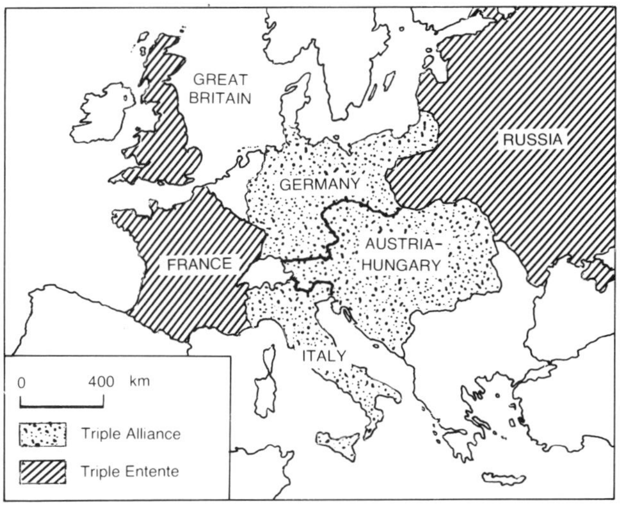

A Europe in 1890 showing the Great Powers and their alliances.

Bismarck had also signed an agreement with Russia called a 'Re-insurance Treaty'. In 1891 the Re-insurance Treaty was due to be renewed, but Kaiser Wilhelm II believed he had no need for Russian friendship and so did not renew the Treaty. Russia, like France, now felt alone.

● *Franco-Russian Alliance*

Fear of Germany forced France and Russia together and in 1892 they signed an alliance – the Franco-Russian Alliance. This stated that:

C If France is attacked by Germany, Russia shall use all her forces to attack Germany. If Russia is attacked by Germany, or by Austria supported by Germany, France shall attack Germany.

Franco-Russian Alliance (1892)

France began to lend large amounts of money to Russia to pay for the building of factories and railways. French money also helped Russia to buy weapons. Russia would soon have an army larger than that of Germany.

B Tsar Nicholas II of Russia blessing his soldiers.

The End of Britain's Isolation

Unlike France and Russia, Britain did not feel threatened by the Triple Alliance. In fact, the opposite was true:

D In 1892 trouble was expected from France and Russia. The solid, quiet group in Europe was the Triple Alliance of, Germany, Austria-Hungary and Italy

Sir Edward Grey (1911)

By the end of the nineteenth century Britain was the only Great Power which had not joined an alliance, although she had clearly given it some thought:

E We do not wish to remain permanently isolated in Europe, and I think that the natural alliance is between ourselves and the great German Empire.

Joseph Chamberlain (1898)

However, when Britain wanted to discuss membership of the Triple Alliance with Germany, she was ignored. Then during the Boer War the Kaiser threatened Britain. First he tried to organise an alliance against Britain, then he commanded building to begin on a huge navy for Germany. Britain began to look elsewhere for friends.

The Triple Entente

In 1904, both Britain and France recognised that they feared Germany more than they feared each other. Arguments between the two over their Empires were settled and an agreement was signed in which they promised to co-operate. This agreement was called the Entente Cordiale.

Encouraged by France, Britain and Russia ended their quarrels over colonies (Persia and Afghanistan) and an agreement was signed by all three. This was the Triple Entente.

F A British cartoon on the Entente Cordiale – The caption read 'Let Germany be careful now'.

Two Armed Camps

By 1908 Europe was firmly divided into two armed camps. On one side stood the Triple Alliance and on the other the Triple Entente. Bismarck's greatest fear had come to pass. The Kaiser's rash actions and threatening manner had united Britain, France and Russia against Germany.

?

1. Why had Bismarck kept France without an ally?
2. What did Russia and France agree to in 1892 according to the evidence in source C?
3. According to sources D and E, why did Britain consider joining the Triple Alliance?
4. What does source F tell us about the *Entente Cordiale*?
5. In your own words explain what the 'two armed camps' were. Use the sources and the text to help you.

THE FIRST MOROCCAN CRISIS (1905–6)

Stung into action by the signing of the *Entente Cordiale* in 1904, Kaiser Wilhelm II went to Tangier in Morocco. His government hoped that a crisis over Morocco would revive the traditional hostility towards each other felt by Britain and France. France would see that Britain was an unreliable ally and the *Entente Cordiale* would be destroyed. The Kaiser's visit was a brief one – just long enough for him to challenge French authority in Morocco in a speech to the Sultan. Morocco should be independent, said the Kaiser, and an international conference must meet to discuss its future. France did not agree.

G Every means was used by Germany to make France understand that if she refused the conference there would be war. France was quite unprepared for war as their army was in a bad state. Russia too was incapacitated.

Winston Churchill (1933) – The Great War, *(Volume 1)*

Under the terms of their alliance of 1892, France could have called on the support of Russia if she was attacked by Germany. However, Germany had timed its move perfectly. In 1905 Russia was defeated in war by Japan and was then paralysed by revolution. France must deal with Germany without her ally. As German threats grew louder, France agreed to a conference. This met in the Spanish town of Algeciras in January 1906. From this point, events turned against Germany. Not only did the conference support French rights in Morocco, but Germany also failed in her chief purpose: destruction of the Anglo-French Entente.

H The Kaiser visiting Tangier, 1905. He is riding a white horse in the middle of the crowd.

Indeed, the Kaiser and his government had made matters worse. The aggression shown by Germany towards France did indeed encourage Britain to reconsider the *Entente Cordiale* – however, not with a view to weakening it, as the Kaiser had hoped, but in order to strengthen it.

I The Great Powers almost went to war over **Morocco.**

SOLID.

GERMANY. "DONNERWETTER! IT'S ROCK. I THOUGHT IT WAS GOING TO BE PAPER."

J This *Punch* cartoon shows German attempts to destroy the *Entente Cordiale*.

K The Prime Minister authorized the beginning of military conversations between the British and French general staffs with a view to concerted action in the event of war. This was a step of profound significance and of far-reaching importance.

Winston Churchill (1933)

THE MATCH-MAKER MALGRÉ ELLE.

MLLE. LA FRANCE (*aside*). "IF SHE'S GOING TO GLARE AT US LIKE THAT, IT ALMOST LOOKS AS IF WE MIGHT HAVE TO BE REGULARLY ENGAGED."

L Britain and France plan to establish closer links despite German disapproval.

The Kaiser's unwise actions had driven France and Britain together. In 1898 they had been on the point of war with each other; by 1906 they had settled their differences and were preparing for war against him.

Germany was surrounded by countries united by their common fear of German aggression. While the Kaiser complained of 'encirclement', his army chief was left to consider how best to fight a war between Germany and the Entente Powers.

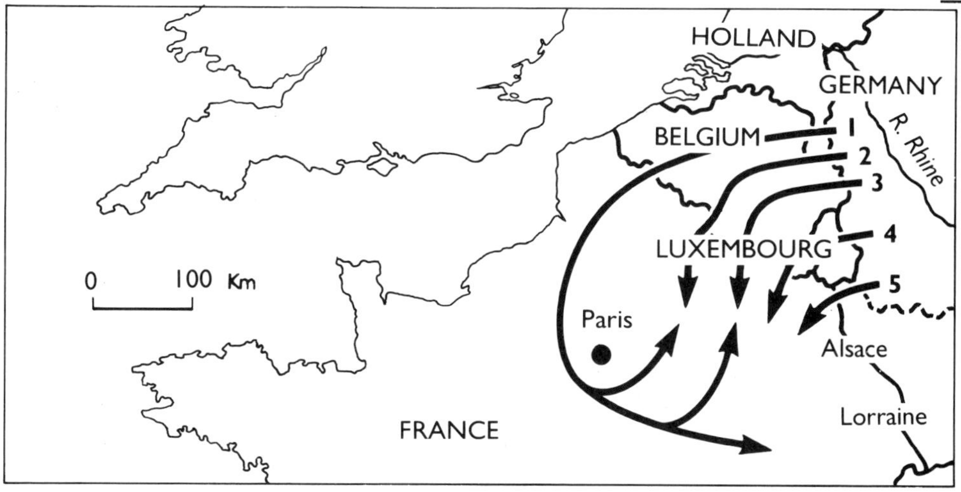

M The Schlieffen Plan (1905) was Germany's plan for winning a war against France and Russia.

The Schlieffen Plan

In December 1905 Count Alfred von Schlieffen, the head of the German army, produced his plan. Since he believed Germany could not win a war on two fronts, he decided not to divide his great army to fight in the East and West simultaneously. Instead von Schlieffen planned:

N . . . to hurl the whole of Germany against one opponent, the one who is strongest, most powerful, most dangerous. This cannot but be France-Britain. The Russian army will be unable to march before matters have been decided in the West.

Count Alfred von Schlieffen (1905)

Von Schlieffen stressed that speed was essential. The signal for the German army to march against France would be the Russian order to its army to mobilise. Russian mobilisation would take six weeks, he guessed, and so, within six weeks, France must be crushed. Once accomplished, the German army would be rushed by train to meet a Russian invasion from the East.

By 1906, plans for war were well advanced. The sides were picked, tactics were being discussed and the venue decided. The Schlieffen Plan meant that the first leg would be fought in France and Belgium, with a second leg somewhere on the Russo-German border.

?

1 Using sources G, H, I and the text, how serious a threat to peace were the Kaiser's actions in 1905–6?

2 What is source J saying about the *Entente Cordiale* and Germany's reaction to it?

3 With a partner study cartoon L.
(a) Which countries are represented in this cartoon?
(b) Give two reasons why the elderly lady is looking on in a disapproving manner.
(c) The cartoonist has labelled the elderly lady as 'the matchmaker'. What effect does this suggest her disapproval is having on the couple's relationship?
(d) How accurately does this cartoon describe the effects of the Moroccan crisis of 1905–6?

4 Using sources K, M, N and the text, describe how the Moroccan crisis increased international tension.

5 **Role Play**: With partner(s), choose *one* of the following and re-enact or write a script for the scene outlined.
(a) Britain, France and Russia discuss why they formed the Triple Entente.
(b) Count von Schlieffen and the Kaiser discuss the German war plan.
(c) Britain and France discuss the Moroccan crisis.

4 NAVAL RIVALRY

As an island power with a large overseas empire, Britain depended on the navy for the safety of its trade and empire. It also protected Britain from invasion – especially important when other Great Powers had far larger armies. As Winston Churchill said

A The purpose of the British navy is purely defensive.

Winston Churchill (1914) – First Lord of the Admiralty

British control of the seas was not challenged until 1898. In that year, Kaiser Wilhelm II decided to make Germany a naval power, when he declared

B The future of Germany lies on the water.

Kaiser Wilhelm II (1898)

This decision meant that Britain could no longer consider an alliance with Germany. Furthermore, Britain's policy of keeping a navy larger in size than any two other navies combined meant that Britain and Germany were now involved in naval competition.

Dreadnoughts

By 1904, the German Kaiser was calling himself 'Admiral of the Atlantic' and Britain had begun to respond to the German challenge. While Admiral Tirpitz supervised the growth of the German navy, Sir John Fisher began re-organising the British navy. He introduced many changes, none more important than the launch, in 1906, of HMS *Dreadnought*.

C British battle cruisers were based in Scotland, across the North Sea from Germany.

D HMS *Dreadnought* – This ship could sink an old-style navy on its own!

In 1906 Britain had far more battleships than Germany, but the launch of HMS *Dreadnought* cancelled out this lead because it was so powerful. Now both countries raced to build Dreadnoughts.

E Dreadnoughts built in Britain and Germany, 1906–14

Date	Britain	Germany
1906	1	0
1907	3	0
1908	2	4
1909	2	3
1910	3	1
1911	5	3
1912	3	2
1913	7	3
1914	3	1

From Craig Mair (1982) – Britain at War

The British people were very concerned at the building of the German navy. Winston Churchill, asked the question on everyone's lips.

F What did Germany want this great navy for? Against whom, except us, could she use it? There was a deep and growing feeling that the Germans meant mischief . . . Moreover, we realised that reluctance on our part to build ships would be seen by Germany as a sign of weakness

Winston Churchill (1933)

PUNCH, OR THE LONDON CHARIVARI.—JANUARY 8, 1908.

POKER AND TONGS;

OR, HOW WE'VE GOT TO PLAY THE GAME.

KAISER. "I GO THREE *DREADNOUGHTS*."

JOHN BULL. "WELL, JUST TO SHOW THERE'S NO ILL-FEELING, I RAISE YOU THREE."

G Britain and Germany raise the stakes in the naval race.

The Kaiser did little to calm British fears. In 1908, with Germany about to increase further the size of its navy, Britain proposed a deal. The Kaiser, however, was in a determined mood:

H If England will only offer the hand of friendship on condition that we limit our navy, it is an absolute cheek, which is a thorough insult to the German people and its Kaiser. If they want war, they can start it, we shall give them what they are asking for!

Kaiser Wilhelm II (1908)

The Kaiser had already stated why he thought Germany had to have a great navy:

I We must have naval power . . . When we have settled our accounts with France and with Russia, will come the last and greatest settlement of accounts – with Great Britain.

Kaiser Wilhelm II (1897)

?

1 (a) Use the text and source A. Why was it important for Britain to have a large navy?
  (b) How did rivalry between Britain and Germany begin?

2 According to source E, who had won the naval race by 1914?

3 How does source G show the naval rivalry between Britain and Germany?

4 (a) Describe Britain's reaction to the growth of the German navy using sources C, D, E and G.
  (b) According to source F, why did Churchill believe that Britain should build ships in competition with Germany?

5 Read sources H and I. Did the Kaiser believe that Germany and Britain would go to war? Give reasons for your answer.

THE SECOND MOROCCAN CRISIS (1911)

In 1908 Germany launched the first of its Dreadnought-type battleships, *The Westfalen*. This caused great concern in Britain and, when the Kaiser tried to calm British fears, he simply increased them. In an interview in the *Daily Telegraph*, he said that the English were stupid not to recognise his friendship at a time when most Germans were 'not friendly' to England.

J *The Westfalen* – the launch of this battleship alarmed the British public.

K Kaiser Wilhelm II claimed that 'The English are as mad as March hares.'

This caused an outcry, both in Britain and in Germany. The German Chancellor, bitterly angry at the Kaiser's conduct, offered to resign.

L All the warnings, all the dismal prophecies of the man he had dismissed from office, Bismarck, returned to people's minds. A dark foreboding ran through many Germans that such incautious, over-hasty, stupid, even childish behaviour on the part of the Kaiser could lead only to one thing – catastrophe.

Prince von Bülow (1908)

The Kaiser was shocked by reactions to his comments and considered abdicating. After this, although naval building went on at pace, there was a period of relative calm. Then, in July 1911, Europe was again plunged into crisis over Morocco.

M Suddenly and unexpectedly, the German Emperor sent his gunboat 'Panther' to Agadir, to maintain and protect German interests in Morocco. All the alarm bells throughout Europe began to ring. Great Britain . . . began to wonder what effect a German naval base on the Atlantic coast of Africa would have on her maritime security, her food routes and trade routes. France was genuinely alarmed. It was difficult to work out what was the real purpose behind the German action. Was Germany looking for an excuse for war with France, or merely trying by pressure and uncertainty to improve her colonial position?

Winston Churchill (1933)

On 21 July 1911, a leading British politician, David Lloyd George, made a speech in London. His speech spelled out how Britain viewed the current crisis in Morocco.

N If a situation were to be forced upon us in which peace could only be preserved by allowing Britain to be treated as if she were of no importance, then I say emphatically that peace at that price would be a humiliation intolerable for a great country like ours to endure.

Lloyd George (1911)

The German government was stunned by Lloyd George's speech as he was thought to be one of Britain's main peace campaigners. The Kaiser was forced to back down, faced with the threat of war, and had to accept that the Entente Cordiale had again stood firm over Morocco.

Worsening Anglo-German Relations

By November 1911 feeling against Britain was running high in Germany. It was to Britain that Heydebrand referred when he made the following speech in the Reichstag:

O Now we know where our enemy stands. Like a flash of lightning in the night, these events have shown the German people where its enemy is. The German people now knows when it seeks its place in the sun, when it seeks the place allotted to it by destiny, where the State is which thinks that it can decide this matter . . . When the hour of decision comes we are prepared for sacrifices, both of blood and of treasure.

Heydebrand (1911)

P Here a German cartoonist shows 'mailed fist' diplomacy at work.

This speech was met with thunderous applause. But, while the Kaiser and others shared this view, Admiral Tirpitz insisted that Germany was not yet in a position to force the issue. Once the Kiel Canal was deep enough to allow German Dreadnoughts to pass from the Baltic Sea to the North Sea, then Germany would be ready to challenge Britain. Work on the canal was completed on 23 June 1914.

Q Admiral Tirpitz – He insisted that Germany should not go to war until mid-1914.

Meanwhile, Britain and France drew closer together. Under the 1912 Anglo-French Naval Convention, the French fleet withdrew to the Mediterranean, while British warships left the Mediterranean for the North Sea. Britain was now obliged to defend the French coast from German attack. As one historian has put it, 'The Entente was coming to look suspiciously like an alliance.'

?

1. What were the main features and the key events of this 'naval arms race' between Britain and Germany?
2. Use sources K, L and M to explain how the Kaiser's actions led to worsening relations between Britain and Germany from 1908.
3. In what ways does the cartoonist (source P) show the Kaiser's strong views on Morocco?
4. Study sources N, O and Q and the text. How close to war were Britain and Germany by 1912?

5 THE BALKANS

Russia and the Balkans

Turkey had once ruled this corner of Europe, but the Turkish Empire was in decline and new nations, such as Serbia and Bulgaria, had appeared. These countries had won the right to govern themselves and were proud of their independence. But two other great empires wanted to control the Balkans. Rivalry between the Russian Empire and the Austro-Hungarian Empire over the Balkans was a cause of the First World War.

The Russian Empire contained many Slavs and they thought that Russia should protect them in the Balkans. The interest shown in the Balkans by Austria-Hungary was therefore resented. The Russian view was that:

A . . . In the Balkans there can only be the Turks or ourselves.

Serge Sazonov (1912)

Austria-Hungary and the Balkans

The Austro-Hungarian Empire also contained Slavs, as well as people of ten other nationalities. The Austrians were afraid that these people might copy the nationalists in the Balkans and demand independence. This would destroy the Austro-Hungarian Empire.

It was clear to the Austrian government that the survival of their Empire depended on stamping out nationalism and those who encouraged it. Austria found Slav nationalism most worrying, especially the growing power of Serbia – the largest Slav country. Serbia wanted to govern all Slavs and so hoped to bring the neighbouring lands of Bosnia-Herzegovina under its control. In 1908, these hopes were dashed.

B 'War will come about over some damned foolish thing in the Balkans,' predicted Bismarck.

C Austria feared that nationalism would destroy her Empire.

● *Bosnian Crisis 1908*

D Austria without warning, took over the Slav provinces of Bosnia and Herzegovina. The Serbians called up their army. But it was the effect on Russia which was most serious. Russians now bitterly hated Austrians and this became a cause of the Great War.

Winston Churchill (1933) – The World Crisis *(Volume 1)*

Serbia and Russia were angry at Austrian action and both considered going to war with Austria.

E Austria decided that Serbia must accept that Bosnia and Herzegovina were now Austrian. If they did not, then Austria would send an ultimatum and declare war upon her. At this point Germany intervened and insisted Russia should advise Serbia to give way. Russia was to agree to this without informing the British or French governments.

Winston Churchill (1933)

Faced with this threat, both Serbia and Russia gave in. Both promised that one day they would seek revenge. Germany and Austria were still unhappy. Germany had hoped that this crisis would destroy the Triple Entente but, instead, this agreement had been strengthened. Although they had won, Austria immediately regretted not having taken the opportunity to crush Serbia completely.

F In this French cartoon Austria is shown grabbing Bosnia and Herzegovina. The Bulgarian ruler takes advantage of the confusion to make himself king.

G . . . as soon as we can, we must settle with Serbia. We can be sure of the Kaiser's support.

Archduke Franz-Ferdinand (1908)

H Archduke Franz-Ferdinand, heir to the Austrian throne – little did he suspect that it would be his death which would give Austria the excuse to go to war in 1914.

?

1. From sources A, F and the text, answer the following questions:
   (a) Who once controlled the Balkans?
   (b) Who wanted to control the Balkans?
2. According to source C and the text, why did Austria fear 'nationalism'?
3. With the help of sources D and E, copy and complete this paragraph:

   In 1908 ________ seized Bosnia and Herzegovina. Serbia reacted by summoning her ________. Russia was also very angry.
   At this point ________ stepped in. Germany insisted that ________ should persuade Serbia to give in. Russia was also told not to say anything to her allies who were ________ and ________.
4. Study sources D, E, G and the text. How important to Austria was the support of Germany?
5. Bismarck predicted that war might result from tension in the Balkans (source B). Do you think that he was exaggerating? Give reasons for your answer using sources D, E and G. (You might also use source L in Chapter 4.)

*T*HE PROLOGUE TO THE FIRST WORLD WAR

Planning the Next Move

As soon as the Bosnian crisis ended, the military in Germany and Austria began to make plans. In January 1909 the German Chief of Staff, von Moltke, wrote to his Austrian counterpart, Conrad von Hotzendorf:

I The time will come when the patience of Austria-Hungary in the face of Serb provocation will come to an end. Then there will be no alternative but for her to attack Serbia. I can say to you, with the Kaiser's approval, that, if Austria were to attack Serbia and Russia were to mobilise, Germany too would mobilise her whole army, which for her means at once opening hostilities against France and Russia.

Count von Moltke (1909) – German Chief of Staff

J Conrad von Hotzendorf and Count von Moltke. These were the men who commanded the forces of Austria-Hungary and Germany.

The Austrian Chancellor wrote to the German Chancellor, von Bülow, in February 1909. He claimed that the Russian people were ready to do anything to avoid war, in which case:

K The idea will be to ensure that any military act against Serbia would not be regarded in Russia as an act of aggression. This, I believe, I can manage by attacking Serbia only when their behaviour becomes openly hostile.

Count Berchtold (1909)

L Count Berchtold, the Austrian Chancellor.

Berchtold was mistaken to think that Russia would permit an Austrian attack on Serbia. Indeed, after being humiliated in 1908, Russia took steps to ensure that any action by her in defence of Serbia would be supported by her friends. The Tsar said to the British government, 'We must keep closer and closer.' Increasingly alarmed by Germany, Britain agreed. In 1914 Britain and Russia held discussions on what military help each could give the other in the event of war.

The Balkan Wars

In 1912 the Balkan countries again defeated Turkey and won from them more land. Russia supported the Balkan countries, forcing Turkey to look to Germany and Austria-Hungary for help. The continuing quarrel between Russia and Austria-Hungary encouraged Russia to find out exactly what the terms of their alliance with France meant.

In August 1912, Sazonov asked President Poincaré to say what France would do if Russia went to war with Germany and Austria-Hungary.

M Poincaré emphasized that public opinion in France would not allow his Government to decide on a military action for purely Balkan questions unless Germany intervened. If this happened we shall certainly be able to count on France.

Serge Sazonov (1912)

N Serge Sazonov (Russian Foreign Minister) and Raymond Poincaré (President of France).

The Second Balkan War: The Growing Threat from Serbia

While Russia and France were agreeing how they would react to the threat of war, Germany and Austria-Hungary were renewing their Alliance. Meanwhile, war again erupted in the Balkans. In this war, Serbia again came out best, gaining more territory and doubling in size. Serbia was bigger and stronger in 1913 than it had been in 1908.

O The chances of a victory over Serbia are less favourable for Austria-Hungary than they would have been had we attacked earlier; the one certain thing is that they would grow worse with every year that passed.

Conrad von Hotzendorf (1913)

In 1913, the Austrian Chancellor Bertchtold asked for the support of Germany against Serbia. The Kaiser gave the following clear reply:

P If Austria-Hungary demands something, then the Serbian government MUST yield; if it does not, then Belgrade will be bombarded, and occupied. Of this you can be sure, that I stand behind you, and am ready to draw the sword if ever your action makes it necessary!

Kaiser Wilhelm II (1913)

The Austrian Chancellor observed that, as he spoke, the Kaiser moved his hands towards his sword hilt.

Serbia was, however, in confident mood. Having played the leading role in splitting up the Turkish Empire, she now looked towards the Austro-Hungarian Empire. The Serbian Prime Minister Pasitch is reported as having said;

Q The first round is won, now we must prepare the second against Austria.

R Kaiser Wilhelm II in a typical pose.

?

Group work: Form six groups, each to study one of the following countries: Serbia, Austria-Hungary, Germany, Russia, France and Britain.

1. Re-read all relevant sources and discuss the importance of affairs in the Balkans 1908–13 for your chosen country.
2. In your group, write a report on what was discussed.
3. Report back to the class.

6 SARAJEVO: THE MURDER THAT ROCKED THE WORLD

A Franz Ferdinand and Sophie, his wife, arrive in Sarajevo on the day of the murder.

The Plot

On 28 June 1914, Archduke Franz-Ferdinand and his wife visited Sarajevo, in the Austrian province of Bosnia. Crowds lined the streets to cheer the royal couple. The Austrian government had promised to take care of security arrangements, but there were few soldiers or policemen around. Along the route were members of a terrorist group called the Black Hand which had its base in Serbia. As the royal car slowed at a junction, one of the terrorists, an 18-year-old Serbian called Gavrilo Princip, took his chance.

B I aimed at the Archduke . . . I do not remember what I thought at that moment. I only know that I fired twice, or perhaps several times, without knowing whether I had hit or missed.

Gavrilo Princip at his trial (1914)

Princip's shots were accurate. Both Franz-Ferdinand and his wife were killed. The Archduke's last words were to his wife. He cried, 'Sophie, Sophie, don't die. Live for the sake of the children.'

The lack of security for the royal visit caused comment:

C I had the impression that Archduke Franz-Ferdinand was sent on purpose to Sarajevo in the hope that this would provoke an incident which might provide Austria with the excuse for war with Serbia.

Leo Pfeffer (1914) – judge at Princip's trial

D Franz Ferdinand's car stops; a few seconds before the assassination.

Serbia on Trial

Princip admitted his guilt, but this was not enough for the Austrian prosecutor. He intended to prove that the Serbian government was involved. Princip denied this.

E Gavrilo Princip – a Slav nationalist.

F This action was our own idea and in no way official as the prosecution suggests. Serbia had no hand in it. No-one else knew of it.

Gavrilo Princip (1914)

Princip must have been convincing because the report of the investigation said:

G There is no proof of the involvement of the Serbian government . . . on the contrary, there are grounds for believing it to be quite out of the question.

But vital evidence had been overlooked. The leader of the Black Hand was the man in charge of the Serbian army. The Serbian government and the Russian government both knew of the plan to assassinate Franz-Ferdinand. But, while the Serbian prime minister had tried to prevent the murders, the Russians had told the Black Hand that they should 'Go ahead' and that Serbia 'will not stand alone'.

● *Reactions*

The death of Franz-Ferdinand came as a relief to many Austrians. He was disliked by the Austrian Emperor, the Prime Minister Count Berchtold and many other leading figures. Now Austria had the excuse they wanted to attack Serbia and they had German support. When the Kaiser heard of the assassination he declared:

H Germany is willing . . . It is high time a clean sweep was made of the Serbs!

Kaiser Wilhelm II (1914)

THE POWER BEHIND.

I This cartoon appeared in *Punch* on 29 July 1914.

?

1 Write a short article for a newspaper in which you describe what happened in Sarajevo on 28 June 1914.

2 (a) Study sources F, G and the text. What lies did Princip tell at his trial?
(b) Who was he trying to protect?
(c) How successful were his lies?

3 Look at source I. Did *Punch* think Serbia had to face Austria alone? Explain your answer.

4 **Group/class discussion:** Who was most to blame for the death of Franz-Ferdinand: Austria, Russia or Serbia?

SERBIA IS PUNISHED

Austria was determined to punish Serbia for the crime committed at Sarajevo, but three weeks passed with no action taken. This lack of urgency by Austria annoyed Germany. One government minister, Alfred Zimmerman, urged Austria to 'act without delay' and cursed the amount of time being spent on 'useless investigations'. The Kaiser, too, insisted that Austria should 'not let the present moment pass'. However, an outright declaration of war by Austria would be considered too strong a reaction by the other Great Powers. Austria had general sympathy and must not lose it. As a first step, therefore, the Austrian government decided to send an ultimatum to Serbia.

J Chancellor Berchtold of Austria gave careful consideration to the wording of the ultimatum.

K Demands must be put to Serbia that would be wholly impossible for them to accept . . . A time limit for the reply must be made as short as possible, presumably forty-eight hours, though even this short time limit would be enough for Serbia to get directions from Russia . . . Were the Serbs to accept all the demands, this would not be to my liking.

Count Berchtold (1914)

Meanwhile, this lull had given President Poincaré of France the opportunity to visit Russia to discuss the present crisis. Austria went to great lengths to find out Poincaré's route.

L President Poincaré of France and Tsar Nicholas II of Russia inspect a guard of Russian sailors at St Petersburg, 22 July 1914.

M Presentation of the ultimatum to Serbia was held back until Monsieur Poincaré had left St Petersburg and was once more on the high seas.

HH Asquith (1923) – The Genesis of War

While at sea, the French leader could not be contacted by either the Russian government or his own. The ultimatum could now be sent. Almost at the same moment, the governments of Britain, Russia and France received a note from the German government. This stated that the German government thought that the demands made of Serbia by the Austrian government were:

N . . . moderate and proper and any interference by Britain, France and Russia would be followed by incalculable consequences.

This threat was issued by the German government before it had seen the text of the Austrian ultimatum. Kaiser Wilhelm, having been sent by his government on a three-week Baltic cruise, knew nothing of these developments. His policies since 1890 had created a recipe for war but by July 1914 he was being pushed aside.

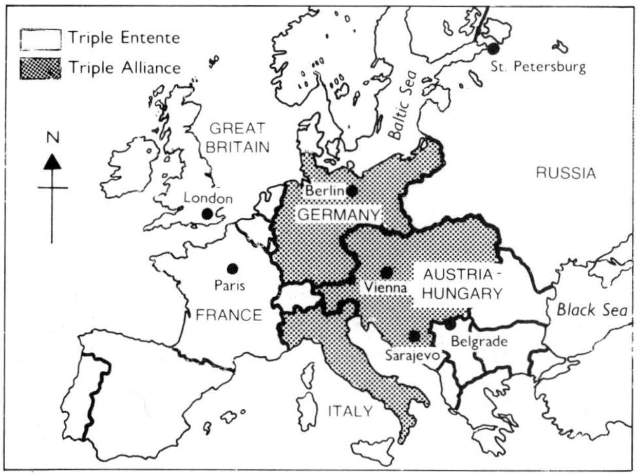

O Europe in 1914.

Serbian Reply

Serbia accepted eight of the ten points of the ultimatum. This amounted to almost total surrender to Austria. When he finally returned from his cruise, the Kaiser was briefed on recent events. On seeing the text of the Austrian ultimatum, he went white. Alarmed at the Kaiser's reaction, Bethmann Hollweg offered to resign. The Kaiser refused to allow it saying:

P You have cooked this broth, now you are going to eat it!

Kaiser Wilhelm II (1914)

Later, when shown a copy of the Serbian reply, the Kaiser's mood changed. He read it enthusiastically:

Q A brilliant achievement in a time limit of only forty-eight hours! It is more than one could have expected! A great moral success for Vienna; but with it all reason for war is gone.

Kaiser Wilhelm II (1914)

The Kaiser then wrote out some ideas which he believed might help prevent war. This plan was to be sent to the government of Austria by the German Chancellor, Herr Bethmann-Hollweg. He held on to this plan until news came through that Austria had declared war on Serbia and commented 'Austria will not be denied her victory'.

The peace plan was then despatched, but too late to do any good. The avoidable delay to this and to other peace proposals being made at the time, led Sir Edward Grey, British Foreign Secretary, to comment, 'There's some devilry going on in Berlin.'

On 28 July, exactly one month after the assassination, the mighty Austro-Hungarian Empire declared war on Serbia.

R Chancellor Bethmann Hollweg of Germany – In July 1914 he blocked attempts to prevent the outbreak of war.

?

1. According to sources K, L and M, how aware was Austria that their ultimatum might lead to war with:
   (a) Serbia?
   (b) Russia?
   (c) France?
2. How far do sources H, N and Q support the view that Germany:
   (a) wanted Austria to attack Serbia?
   (b) was aware that Russia, France and Britain might become involved?
3. A man of peace or a warmonger? In a group decide which view of the Kaiser is correct. You should also use evidence from earlier work.
4. Study all sources in which the Kaiser is associated with boats.
   (a) What changes are evident in his status and influence?
   (b) On page 4 the Kaiser is shown taking command of the ship *Germany*. Draw a cartoon and write a suitable caption to describe his position in July 1914.

7 A WAR THAT NOBODY WANTED

On 28 July 1914, Austria attacked Serbia. Next day, the Russian army was mobilised to defend Serbia. A Russian diplomat recalled the signing of the mobilisation order.

A The Tsar was deadly pale and spoke in a choking voice.

Maurice Paleologue (1923)
An Ambassador's Memoirs *vol 1*

Austria, now threatened by Russia, looked to her ally Germany for the promised assistance. On 1 August Germany sent an ultimatum to Russia warning her to cancel mobilisation. The deadline was noon but by 4.00 pm Germany had received no reply. Falkenhayn, the German War Minister acted.

B The Chancellor and I drove to see the Kaiser to ask him to sign the mobilisation order. After considerable resistance he consented. Once he had signed, the Kaiser gave me a long hand shake and we both had tears in our eyes.

Erich Falkenhayn (1914)

The German Ambassador to Russia was then told to deliver the declaration of war. Sazonov, the Russian Foreign Minister, was the man who received it.

C After handing the note to me, the German Ambassador lost all self control and leaning against the window burst into tears.

Serge Sazonov (1914)

War between Germany and Russia would also involve France, with whom Russia had an alliance. It was against France that Germany struck first. France had to be defeated within six weeks to enable the transfer of the German army to the East to meet the advancing Russians. Germany's declaration of war on France left Britain as the only Great Power not at war. What would Britain do? Britain had signed no alliances and so need not get involved. When Sir Edward Grey, was asked by the French Ambassador for help, he replied, 'France must not count on our support.' The German Ambassador also visited him. Grey recalled:

D He was very emotional and begged me not to side with France. He said that Germany, with her army cut in two between France and Russia, was likely to be crushed. He was very agitated, poor man and wept.

Sir Edward Grey (1914)

E Sir Edward Grey – He warned Germany that Britain would assist France while advising France that she would not.

The Invasion of Belgium

Germany pressed on with the attack on France. To achieve a quick victory Germany planned to send troops through Belgium. Belgium was a neutral country wishing only to be left in peace. On 2 August, the German government asked Belgium to allow her troops to pass through. Permission was refused.

[Reproduced by permission of the Proprietors of 'Punch.'

BRAVO, BELGIUM!

F A *Punch* cartoon from August 1914.

On 4 August, German troops poured into Belgium. Britain issued an ultimatum to Germany stating that her troops must leave Belgium by midnight, or Britain would go to war with Germany. Lloyd George described how the British government awaited the German reply.

G As midnight approached, a deep and tense solemnity fell on the room. No-one spoke. We awaited the signal to send millions of men to their doom. Our eyes wandered anxiously from the clock to the door, and the door to the clock. Boom! the deep notes of Big Ben rang out and a thrill of horror quickened every pulse.

David Lloyd George (1933) – War Memoirs (Volume 1)

Meanwhile in Germany, Chancellor Bethmann-Hollweg groaned and said:

H A war that nobody wanted is about to be unleashed.

Chancellor Bethmann-Hollweg (1914)

?

1. Using sources A and B, compare the reactions of the Tsar of Russia and the German Kaiser to the outbreak of war.
2. Sources A and G give the same reason why Europe's leaders were upset at this time. What is this reason?
3. Source G describes the British government awaiting a message.
   (a) From whom?
   (b) What did the government hope the message would say?
4. Source C mentions one person who wept when war was declared. Identify three others from other sources who did the same.

Group work

5. Give reasons why F is a useful source for those studying the outbreak of the First World War.
6. Discuss how far you agree with Bethman-Hollweg (source H) that the war now breaking out was 'a war that nobody wanted'.

BRITAIN MUST BE HELD RESPONSIBLE?

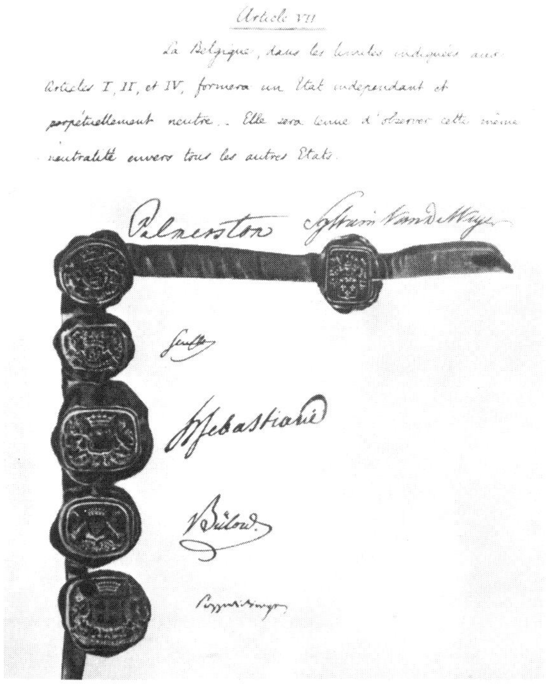

I The Treaty of London 1839 – Britain was one of the signatories.

By signing the Treaty of London, Britain had promised to defend Belgian neutrality, even if that meant going to war. Germany thought Britain was taking this far too seriously, as Bethmann-Hollweg explained to the British Ambassador:

J Just for a word – 'neutrality', a word which in war-time had so often been disregarded – just for a scrap of paper, Great Britain was going to make war on a kindred nation who desired nothing better than to be friends with her . . . what Britain had done was unthinkable; it was like striking a man down from behind whilst he was fighting for his life against two assailants. Britain must be held responsible for the terrible events that might happen.

Bethmann-Hollweg (1914)

Strong feelings were aroused in Britain over the German invasion of neutral Belgium. To many it was not the act of a civilised nation. German hostility to Britain was equally strong. Many leading Germans had not expected Britain to become involved in the war. The Kaiser felt he had been deceived. 'The low down shopkeeping knaves,' he said, 'have been trying to take us in.' Falkenhayn, the German War Minister declared:

K Of course we never expected for one moment that Britain would enter the war . . . the coming in of Britain made all the difference in the world.

Erich Falkenhayn (1914)

When Bethmann-Hollweg learned of Britain's intention to support France and Russia, he immediately contacted the Austrian government:

L In these circumstances we most urgently and emphatically recommend that you settle the dispute with Serbia, or else we will face catastrophe.

Bethmann-Hollweg (1914)

Admiral Tirpitz was another who felt that Germany would have done more to preserve the peace if they had known sooner that Britain might become involved.

M Britain brought upon itself a large share of the responsibility for the outbreak of the war by uncertainty as to its attitude during the crisis. Grey could have preserved peace if he had in time made clear to Bethmann-Hollweg Britain's attitude in the event of the Austro-Serbian conflict spreading to the rest of Europe.

Alfred von Tirpitz (1919)
My Memoirs

This view is also supported by Sazonov.

N A decisive statement on the part of the British government of its solidarity with France had in 1911 been sufficient to dispel the gathering storm clouds. I am convinced now that, had the British government sided with Russia and France on the Serbian question from the first, Berlin would not have encouraged Austria in its policy of aggression but would, on the contrary, have advised caution and moderation.

Serge Sazonov (1927) – Fateful Years

Winston Churchill was of the same opinion:

O Our Entente with France and the military and naval conversations that had taken place since 1906 had given us the obligations of an alliance without its advantages. An open alliance, would have discouraged Germany.

Winston Churchill (1933) –
The World Crisis *(Volume 1)*

INJURED INNOCENCE.

THE GERMAN OGRE. "HEAVEN KNOWS THAT I HAD TO DO THIS IN SELF-DEFENCE; IT WAS FORCED UPON ME." (*Aside*) "FEE, FI, FO, FUM!"

[According to the Imperial Chancellor's latest utterance Germany is the deeply-wronged victim of British militarism.]

P A *Punch* cartoon from 1914.

However, this view was not shared by two people at the centre of events:

Q There is no evidence to prove that a threatening attitude on our part would have turned Germany and Austria from the path on which they had entered. On the contrary the evidence is all the other way. Bethmann-Hollweg himself has ridiculed the idea that Germany made a miscalculation in counting on British neutrality. 'This,' he writes, 'runs counter to the facts.'

Herbert Asquith – British Prime Minister (1908-1915) The Genesis of War *– 1923*

In the Europe of 1914, too few people dreaded the prospect of war. In Russia, and in Austria-Hungary, there were those who saw war as a way to avoid revolution at home. In France, many shared the opinion that never before had war offered itself under such favourable conditions. In Germany, as far back as December 1912, it was decided that the war could begin against the Entente Powers sometime after 23 June 1914. This was the expected date for completion of improvements to the Kiel Canal. It was not only the German navy which favoured war in 1914, but also the army:

R The situation is from the military point of view, favourable to a degree which cannot occur again in the foreseeable future.

Helmuth von Moltke – (1914)
German Chief of Staff

By midnight on 4 August 1914, those who wanted war had their wish. Sir Edward Grey commented, 'The lamps are going out all over Europe. They will not be lit again in our lifetime.'

?

1. Compare cartoons F and P.
   (a) In what ways are they similar?
   (b) In what ways is cartoon P more critical of Germany?
   (c) How could Germany claim to be defending itself?
2. **Role play**
   Form six groups. Each group is to represent one of the following countries: Germany, Austria-Hungary, Russia, France, Britain and Serbia. Each group should study the attitudes and actions of their country in the years before 1914. Each group in turn should make a confession to the class concerning their role in bringing about the First World War. Once each confession has been made, the class can discuss each claim and attribute blame.

8 THE FIRST EXPERIENCE OF WAR – ATTITUDES 1914

On 4 August 1914, a young English girl called Vera Brittain noted this in her diary.

A I am almost too excited to write at the stupendous events of this day – war is declared between France and Germany. Sir Edward Grey's statement that 'we are prepared' got a tremendous cheer in the House [of Commons].

Vera Brittain – Testament of Youth

Later that day as the German invasion of Belgium continued, the British government under Prime Minister Asquith, declared war on Germany and took Britain into the war.

All over Europe there was great excitement when war was declared – after all, there had not been a major war in Europe for nearly a hundred years and in Britain the declaration was greeted with great enthusiasm. Crowds took to the streets waving flags and singing patriotic songs. People danced and cheered outside Buckingham Palace in a wave of patriotism which swept the country in those first days of the war.

Britain though, was only partly ready to fight a war. Britain's strength had always been in its navy, but its army was small. Lord Kitchener, British Secretary of State for War, believing that the war would be long, declared:

B An excited crowd gathered in Trafalgar Square on 4 August. Members of all classes were excited at the prospect of war.

C . . . three years will do to begin with. A nation like Germany, will only give in after it is beaten to the ground. That will be a very long time. No-one living knows how long.

Lord Kitchener (1914)

This view, though, was not popular. Instead, the newspapers preferred to encourage the belief that it would be a short war – over by Christmas at the latest.

Government Action – Recruitment

When war broke out the British army (the British Expeditionary Force) numbered only 150,000 men. In August 1914 they left for Belgium. Kitchener realised that for a long war, the army had to be enlarged and so he called for 100,000 volunteers to form a second army. One of the earliest experiences of war for young British men was to be bombarded with government propaganda aimed at persuading them to volunteer for Kitchener's new army.

D The posters encouraged enlistment through patriotism.

Patriotism

Young men were put under great pressure by families and friends to join up. Posters like sources D and E began to appear and it was soon a disgrace for a young man to be seen in the streets without a uniform. Later in the war there was a campaign by women to disgrace men not in uniform by pinning a white feather (a sign of cowardice) to their jackets.

E The call to 'do your duty' was a powerful influence on young men.

The call to the nation for volunteers was a huge success. Pride and patriotism combined to persuade over 500,000 young men to join the army in the first weeks of the war.

?

Copy and complete questions 1-3.

1. Britain declared war on ________ because ________________ .
2. The people of Britain were ________ about going to war. I know this from sources A and B because ________________ .
3. The B________ E________ F________ was the British army in 1914. It had ________ soldiers in 1914.
4. Why did Britain need to raise a large army in August 1914? Use source C and the text to help you find two reasons.
5. In what way did the poster in (a) source D and (b) source E encourage young men to enlist?
6. What evidence is there that the government's recruitment campaign was a success?

TAKING THE KING'S SHILLING

F Propaganda poster showing the Germans as beasts.

Propaganda

In the first weeks of the war, the government launched a propaganda campaign to encourage enlistment and, indeed, hatred of the Germans. Stories of terrible acts of cruelty by the Germans were reported in the British press – stories of mothers and their children being bayonetted by German soldiers and of innocent villagers being shot without reason. The Germans were shown as beasts and brutal murderers, and, while we still do not know whether these stories were true or invented, they did make many British people determined to fight.

G I never though of joining up but I had an old school mate, Walter, who was very patriotic, and when he heard of the so-called atrocities committed in Belgium, he was so angry that he decided to enlist and dragged me in with him.

Pte G Brownbridge, (13th Northumberland Fusiliers)

In 1914 the most popular form of entertainment was the music hall where patriotic songs were sung and young men were asked to make their mothers proud of them. Songs like 'Your King and Country Want You' became very popular recruiting songs.

Robert Graves, who enlisted in 1914 and eventually rose to the rank of Captain, had another reason for enlisting:

H The papers predicted only a very short war – over by Christmas at the outside. I hoped that it might last long enough to delay my going to Oxford [University] in October which I dreaded.

Robert Graves – Goodbye to All That

Amongst the recruits, however, were many who should not really have been accepted.

The excitement was so great that many young men were prepared to trick their way in.

George Coppard was encouraged to lie by the Recruiting Sergeant in order to be allowed to enlist:

I The sergeant asked me my age and, when told, replied, 'Clear off son. Come back tomorrow and see if you're nineteen.' So I turned up again the next day and gave my age as nineteen . . . I was sixteen years and seven months old.

George Coppard – With a Machine-gun to Cambrai.

J Enlistment by a hairsbreadth! On this occasion the army was prepared to stretch the rules.

K German students celebrate the declaration of war.

Pte. Brownbridge and his friend Walter went along to a recruiting station.

L I was a big lad for my age and was accepted immediately but Walter was an inch too short so he was turned down. He came back a short time later with his shoes stuffed with cardboard and was accepted.

Pte G Brownbridge

Stories of boys and men enlisting in this way were common throughout the country. In some areas, whole streets of men volunteered together and, in Glasgow, the Corporation tramcar drivers and conductors joined as a group. These groups of friends were formed into 'Pals' Battalions' and went off to train together. Later events were to show just what a tragic mistake it was to allow so many from the one neighbourhood to join the same battalion.

War fever had gripped Britain, but the excitement and enthusiasm for battle was the same throughout Europe. French, Belgians, Germans, Russians and Austrians all marched to war believing in the glory of their cause. On 6 August 1914, a young German student wrote to his parents:

M My dear ones, be proud that you live in such times and in such a nation, and that you have the privilege of sending several of those you love into this glorious struggle.

Walter Limmer (1914)

?

1. Compare the views of Kitchener (source C) and Graves (source H) about the length of the war. Whose predictions was most likely to be accurate and why?
2. If Kitchener's view had been more widely known, how and why might they have affected recruitment?
3. Explain why Brownbridge, Graves and Walter joined the army.
4. Why do you think Coppard and Walter cheated to get into the army?
5. Compare the attitudes towards the declaration of war in Britain and Germany.
6. **Class discussion:** What were the reasons why the British government's recruitment campaign was so successful in 1914? You should consider the following: patriotism, the Belgian atrocities, the newspaper predictions, the poster campaign, patriotic songs and propaganda.
7. Write a short essay describing the recruitment campaign and the reasons for its success.

9 MODERN WARFARE

When war broke out in 1914 the generals of all sides expected a war of movement. It was thought that cavalry and infantry charges would destroy the enemy and that victory would be swift. Having masses of men was considered an advantage and it was thought that Russia's millions in the East would roll over the Germans like a steamroller.

In the West, the French and British relied upon the cavalry and infantry. Before 1914, General Haig (who was later to become the Commander of the British Army), had predicted:

A The cavalry will have an important role in future wars.

General Douglas Haig (1914)

Events were to prove him very wrong.

The impact of new technology

By 1914 new technology had been developed for modern armies – big guns capable of accurate shellfire over long distances and machine-guns which were able to fire hundreds of bullets every minute. However, it was the Germans who had . . .

C . . . studied the machine-gun more than other armies and were able to use its power to dominate a battlefield sooner than other armies.

B Liddell-Hart (1970) –
History of World War I

B The machine-gun made brave infantry and cavalry charges across open ground suicidal.

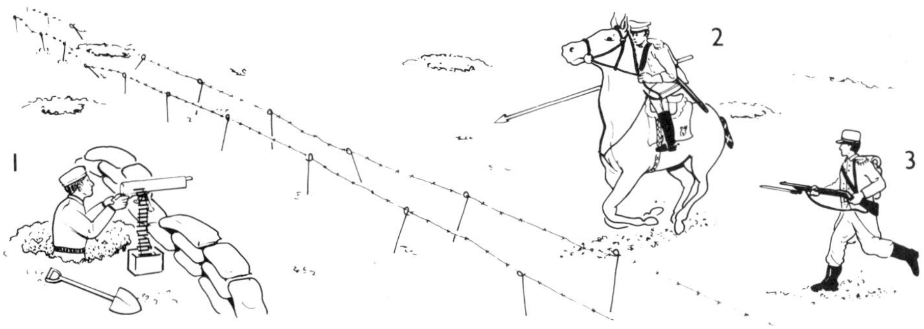

D The modern battlefield.

The French soldiers of 1914 went into battle wearing brightly coloured uniforms and glinting bayonets. Their tactics were to charge towards the German positions courageously with their bayonets at the ready. However, on the fields of Alsace and Lorraine, they were easy and colourful targets for German machine-gunners. They were slaughtered in huge numbers.

The British and French were slower to understand the power of the machine gun, some believing it to be:

E . . . a much over-rated weapon and two per battalion is more than enough.

General Douglas Haig (1914)

● *The power of the machine-gun*

At the start of the war the generals were wrong in how they believed the war would develop. Too many of them still thought that the sabre (sword) of the horseback soldier, the bayonet of the footsoldier and grit and determination would win wars. Too few of them had learned the lessons of previous wars in which the increasing power of weapons had changed the nature of warfare.

Judge for yourself the power of the machine-gun from this incident which took place in 1916.

F The front line jumped up and walked into the open . . . machine-guns from several points sprayed their deadly fire backwards and forwards dropping men like corn before the reaper. In far less time than it takes to write it, the attacking waves became a mere sprinkling of men. They went on for a yard or two and then all seemed to vanish.

Captain Gilbert Nobbs, July 1916

Until the realities of modern warfare became obvious, the generals had all been sure that a swift victory could be achieved and that the enemy would soon be crushed – modern firepower destroyed their hopes.

?

1 One of the soldiers in source D is French, one German and one British. By using sources A,B, and C and the text identify each soldier correctly.

2 Imagine the diagram showed a real event. Which of the soldiers would have the best chance of survival? Give two reasons for your answer.

3 Using source D to help you:
(a) If soldiers had to 'dig in' before attacking towards machine-gunners, this would lead to *long/short* battles. (Choose one of the italicised words.) Give at least one reason for your answer.
(b) If soldiers attacked the machine-gunners in large numbers there would probably be *large/small* numbers of casualties. (Choose one of the italicised words.) Give one reason to explain your answer.

MODERN FIREPOWER

The hail of fire which swept the modern battlefield in 1914 was devastating to soldiers in open ground. The Germans were amongst the machine-gun's first casualties at Liege in Belgium. A Belgian officer witnessed this scene.

G They came on, line after line, almost shoulder to shoulder, until, as we shot them down, the fallen were heaped one on top of the other in an awful barricade of dead and wounded. It was slaughter – just slaughter.

J Terraine – White Heat

In Alsace and Lorraine the French 'Plan 17' ended in similar disaster:

H The sense of the tragic futility of it will never quite fade from the minds of those who saw these brave men, dashing across the open ground to the sound of bugles and drums, clad in old red caps and trousers. The gallant officers who led them were entirely ignorant of the stopping power of modern firearms.

Sir Edward Spears

As one soldier commented, by 1914 . . .

I . . . The safety of a man so often depends upon his handling of his spade; the deeper a man digs, the better is his shelter from bullet and bomb. The spade is the key to safety.

Patrick McGill – The Big Push

J The armies of 1914 were supported by artillery fire from guns which were increasing in size and effectiveness.

Artillery gunners also added to the hail of fire. The guns rained down massive doses of high explosive and shrapnel on the infantry. In contests between man and metal there was only one winner.

By September the various war plans had failed – Plan 17, the Schlieffen Plan, the Russian 'Steamroller' – and all of them had ended with enormous casualties. French losses by the end of August 1914 alone were a staggering 211,000 officers and men either dead or wounded and it is estimated that the German experience was as bad, if not worse, as they were fighting on two fronts. The spade now became the key to safety and troops from all of the warring nations dug trenches to protect themselves from the effects of modern technology.

Stalemate

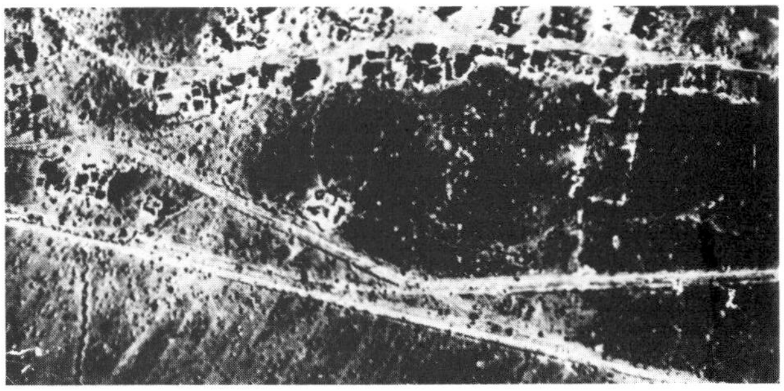

K The parallel rows of trench lines as seen from the air. No-man's land can be clearly seen.

From September 1914, the war of movement came to an end and the rival armies found themselves in parallel rows of trenches, separated by a belt of disputed territory known as 'no-man's land' – in some places 'a thousand yards wide', in others only a few yards. This type of warfare and its implications had been predicted in 1890 by a Polish banker but the Generals had paid no heed to his prophetic warnings.

L Everybody will be entrenched in the next war. The spade will be as indispensable to a soldier as his rifle . . . It will be impossible for the battle of the future to be fought out rapidly. All digging work is slow work and when you must dig a trench before you can make any advance, your progress is necessarily slow. Battles will last for days and at the end it is very doubtful whether any decisive victory can be gained.

Ivan Bloch (1890)

M Razor-sharp wire – the stumbling block.

Bloch's predictions came true in 1914. From that time onwards, the generals of both sides were faced with a problem – forward progress without high casualties was impossible – but there could be no victory without forward movement. All governments challenged their industries to develop technology which could overcome the stalemate.

● *1915 – Gas*

On 22 April 1915 a member of the Queen Victoria Rifles witnessed the following scene:

N We could see the flash of shrapnel and a low cloud of yellow-grey smoke or vapour. In the northerly breeze came a pungent and sickening smell that tickled the throat and made the eyes smart. Over the fields streamed mobs of infantry . . . away went their rifles, equipment, even tunics that they might run faster.

Anthony Hossack (Queen Victoria Rifles)

The Germans had released chlorine gas. The Algerian and French troops who were holding that part of the line fled in panic and a gap of some four miles opened up in the Allies' defences. The Germans, though, did not follow up the attack and they lost their advantage. The warnings were immediately heeded and led to the swift introduction of counter-measures.

The early masks were quite crude, as one soldier explained:

O They consisted of a piece of muslin with a pad of cotton wool. In the event of a gas attack, we were told to urinate on the pad and bind it to our mouth and nose.

Anthony Hossack (1915)

P Gas masks.

The masks became more sophisticated and, while the use of chlorine, phosgene and mustard gases had horrific consequences, gas did not prove to be the decisive weapon.

?

1. Describe the effects of the machine-gun at Liege and Alsace-Lorraine.
2. On what did Ivan Bloch and Patrick McGill agree concerning modern warfare. How had new technology brought this about?
3. What effects would entrenchments have on war, according to Bloch?
4. How do sources K and M support Bloch?
5. Describe the impact of gas in April 1915. Explain why gas was not the decisive weapon of the war.

10 TRENCH WARFARE

The British view of trenches was summed up by George Coppard:

A Our trench warfare seemed to be based upon the idea that we were not stopping in the trenches for long, and that very soon we would be chasing Jerry across country. The result was that we lived in lousy scratch holes.

George Coppard – With a Machine-gun to Cambrai

Instead of temporary trenches, the Germans built a strong network of trench lines to hold on to what they had taken.

Conditions at the front

The trench system proved so difficult to break through that the soldiers of both sides were camped opposite each other for four years. Living outdoors in all weathers in summer and in winter was uncomfortable and unpleasant. When the ground was torn up by constant artillery fire, conditions simply got worse and worse.

C Flanders is just one great bog. Day and night we stand up to our knees in mud and water. On top of this, the mad gun-battle goes on in front of us and it is dangerous even to raise your head above ground during the day.

Friedrich Nickolas (December 1915)

The dirt and filth of the trenches encouraged rats and lice. 'Corpse rats' fed on the bodies of dead soldiers.

D The rats were very thorough.

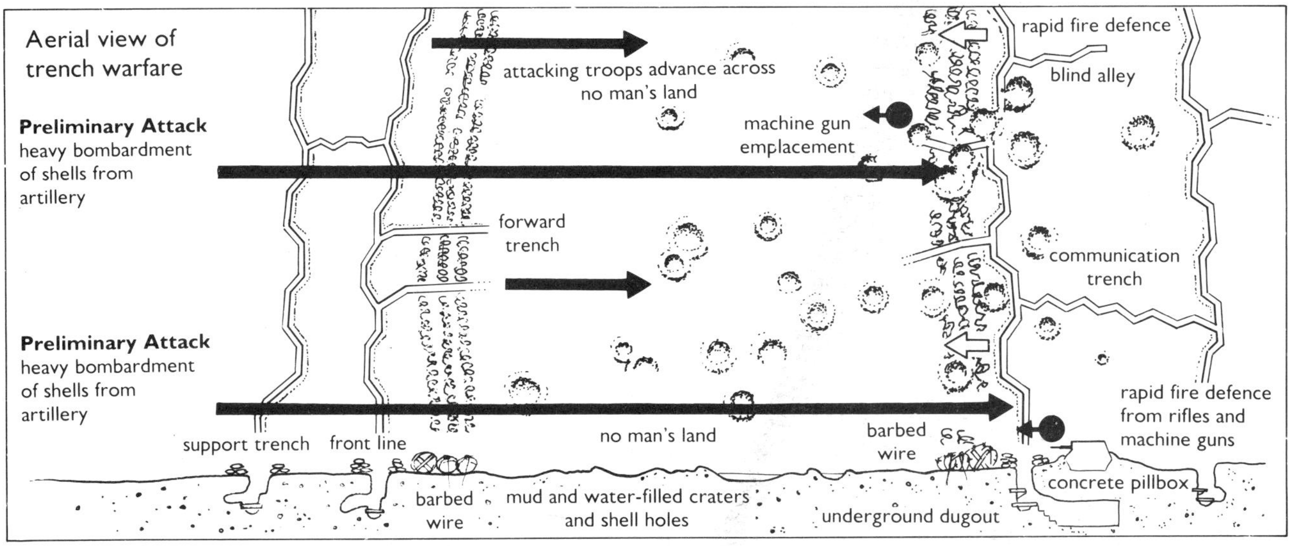

B A typical trench system showing two defensive lines, the wire and no-man's land.

Body lice were also a constant nuisance but first hand accounts sometimes contain amusing stories about these pests.

E I had raided a house and found a pair of ladies' bloomers. I thought it would be a good idea to get rid of my skin-tight pants and wear these instead, but I soon discovered that I had made a bad mistake. With more room to move about, the lice swarmed into those bloomers in platoons and in a few days I was the lousiest man in the company.

Frank Richards – Old Soldiers Never Die

Routine work

Damaged trenches and wire had to be constantly repaired. This was often dangerous work as snipers were always on the lookout for unwary soldiers. A British soldier, Frank Bastable, recalled this story about the death of his friend Bill Beckington in August 1915.

F We hadn't been in the line long. Bill and I were told to go up and repair a trench. When we got there he said, 'I'll go up. You fill the bags and hand them up to me.' But as soon as he went up there was a shot, and Bill was hit in the head. I can still see it now, bits of his brains on my tunic. Poor Bill, they should have told us.

Frank Bastable – The Somme

G German sniping team with spotter and killer.

Life in the front-line trenches was uncomfortable and dangerous. For some soldiers the strain was too much and soldiers of both sides sometimes gave up. A British officer came across a man in a dug-out:

H I shook him by the arm and noticed a hole in the back of his head. He had taken off the boot and sock to pull the trigger of his rifle with one toe; the muzzle was in his mouth.

Robert Graves – Goodbye to All That

I The German artist Otto Dix shows that Germans also committed suicide.

?

1 Which of the sources say that:
(a) it was dangerous to raise your head above ground level?
(b) trench warfare was too much for some soldiers?

2. Why are eyewitness accounts useful to historians studying conditions in the trenches? **Consider** (a) who the authors were; (b) whether the sources agree about conditions; (c) the photographic evidence.

TRYING TO BREAK THE DEADLOCK

J Even in a trench the soldiers were vulnerable to artillery bombardments – and in any case, sitting still would not win the war.

The main problem with trench warfare was highlighted by Ian Hay:

K The fact is, a trench is neither satisfactory as a home nor efficient as a weapon of offence. The knowledge that you are reasonably safe from the attacks of your enemy is discounted by the fact that he is equally safe from yours.

Ian Hay (1915) – The First Hundred Thousand

The simple truth was that the war would not be won by remaining in the trenches and, while the Germans were camped on French soil, it was necessary for the British and French to remain on the offensive. Where gas had failed, perhaps the big guns could succeed.

Artillery – The 'God of War'

As the armies had stopped moving it became possible to use large, fairly immobile guns, against the enemy positions and to concentrate fire along short sections of the front line in an attempt to pierce the line. In May 1915, General Ferdinand Foch launched an offensive in Artois towards Vimy Ridge. Before he sent his infantry to battle, Foch ordered a massive bombardment of the German positions in an attempt to kill the defending Germans and to destroy the wire. From then onwards, artillery was to become the 'God of War'.

Gunnery techniques improved during the war as there were fewer losses amongst the gunners. With the help of aerial spotting and improvements in range-finding and accuracy, the artillery became more effective. By 1916, no-one was in any doubt about the power of the guns. A soldier under fire at Verdun in that year wrote:

L We instantly recognise the shell that is coming to bury us. As soon as we pick out its dismal howl we look at each other in agony. All curled and shrivelled up we crouch . . . we stagger about like drunks. The beams tremble, a cloud of choking smoke fills the dug-out, the candles go out.

Jacques l'Arnoux quoted in White Heat *by J Terraine*

M The increasing use and concentration of the guns.

Date	Battle	Heavy Guns	Front (miles)	Guns/ mile
1916	Somme	452	14	32
1917	Ypres	575	3	192
1918	Arras	963	13	71
1918	Vimy Ridge	377	4	94

The statistics for Verdun in 1916 are even more awesome. During the course of the battle over 1000 shells were fired for every square metre of the battlefield and the total casualties for that battle alone in 1916 was more than 700,000 French and Germans.

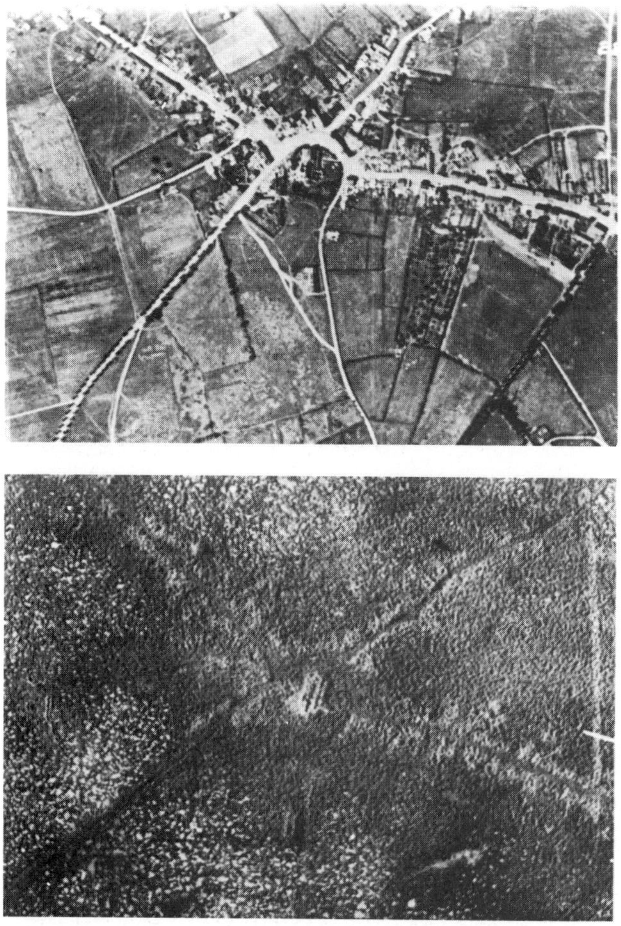

N The 'God of War' brought destruction and death. The effects of concentrated artillery fire are all too obvious to see in these aerial photographs of the Passchendaele battlefield.

Artillery caused the highest number of casualties in the war – more than the machine-gun and rifle – and the types of wounds were often horrific. Explosions often buried soldiers alive in their dug-outs and many soldiers were literally blown to pieces by shells. There was little protection against the big guns except to dig down deeper and deeper and, in some sectors along the Western Front, dug-outs were as deep as 9–12 metres and reinforced with concrete.

As well as having dug-outs, the soldiers of all armies were eventually issued with steel helmets, since a very high percentage of deaths occurred from shrapnel head wounds. However, there was some opposition to this from one British general who believed it would make them soft.

The big guns then, despite their power, could not win a quick, decisive victory. Deep underground, soldiers could find some protection and the shelling often simply threw the barbed wire into the air only to tangle it worse than before on landing. The generals came to see that, if the stalemate could not be broken by the guns, at least they could be used to wear down the enemy's numbers. However, in the summer of 1916, the British still placed great faith in the power of the big guns at the Somme.

O The remains of a shallow German dug-out after an artillery attack.

?

1. Using appropriate sources, explain why conditions in the trenches led to suicides.
2. What was the main problem with trench warfare according to Ian Hay?
3. Describe the effects of an artillery bombardment using sources L,M,N and O.
4. (a) What counter-measures were taken against artillery?
   (b) Why could artillery not achieve a quick victory?
5. Find out what is meant by a war of attrition.

11 THE BATTLE OF THE SOMME

A A heavy gun opens up at the Somme.

On 1 July 1916, the British launched a mass attack on a twenty mile front of the German line north of the River Somme. For the attack, they gathered together 452 heavy guns, 1,500,000 shells, 185 aeroplanes, 14 observation balloons, dug mines under the German lines and assembled a human battering ram of 519,000 soldiers.

The British thought that the success of the attack depended on the artillery. They believed that after the pounding they had planned for the German trenches, no German soldier would be left alive and the enemy wire and artillery would both be destroyed. As an eyewitness noted:

B While the guns were blazing, when we saw what was happening to the German trenches we all had our tails up. We thought nothing could survive the bombardment.

Bill Partridge (7th Middlesex Regiment)

C The ear splitting bark of the eighteen pounders, the cough of the howitzers, the boom of the heavy guns . . . it was wonderful music – the mightiest I ever heard . . . one felt inclined to laugh at the sheer excitement of it all.

Lt. Adrian Stephen

The guns opened up on 24 June and the sound of the exploding shells could be heard in London. To the British troops, who had seen the war become a frustrating slog in the trenches, it seemed that things were about to take a more exciting turn:

The plan had not been properly thought out, however. The artillery had used shrapnel shells, which exploded in the air sending down a shower of lead balls. They did not break the barbed wire. British troops, moving slowly forward across No-Man's Land, found the German wire impossible to pass through and were mown

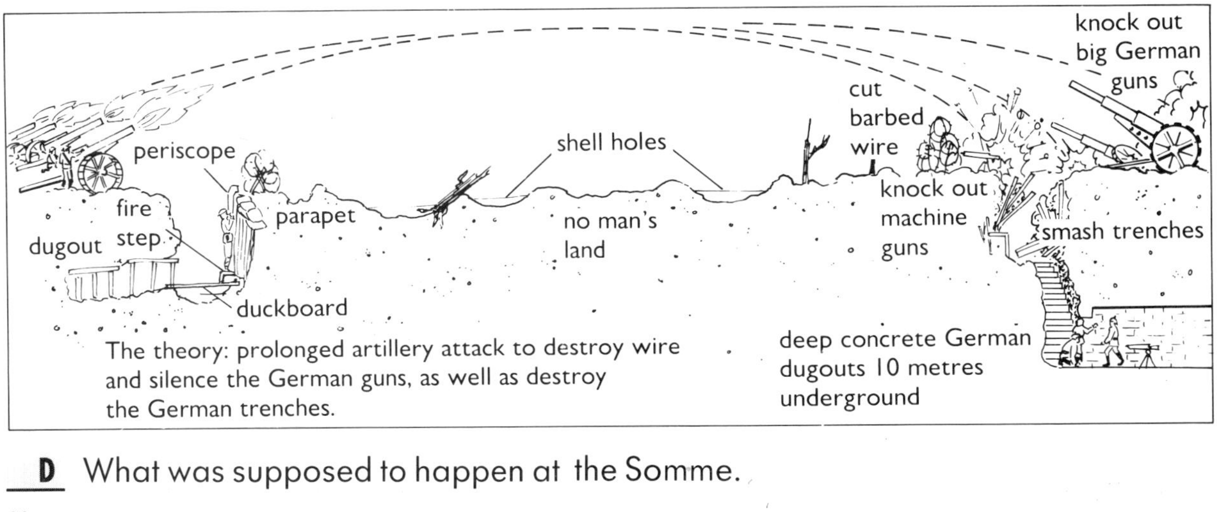

D What was supposed to happen at the Somme.

E What actually happened at the Somme.

down by the Germans who had, for the most part, been hiding safely in deep dugouts and had emerged with their machine guns when the shelling stopped. As one bitter veteran of the Somme has said:

F How did the planners imagine that British soldiers would get through the wire? Who told them that the artillery would pound it to pieces? Any Tommy could have told them that shellfire lifts wire up and drops it down, often in a worse tangle than before.

G Coppard

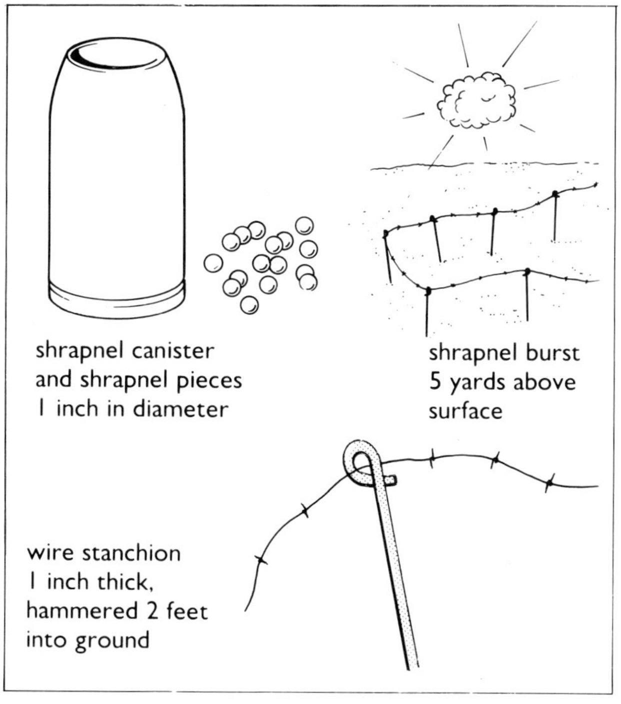

G The plan to burst the wire.

The attack was a terrible disaster. Whole units were wiped out as they probed for a way through the wire. On the first day of the Battle of the Somme, the blackest day in the history of the British army, 20,000 British soldiers were killed and 37,000 wounded or taken prisoner.

?

1. Copy this paragraph and fill in the blanks using the information on these two pages.

   The British had gathered together ______ soldiers to attack the German positions on the River ______. They believed that the artillery would kill the German ______ and destroy the German ______ and ______. The plan failed, mostly because the artillery did not destroy the ______. 20,000 British soldiers were killed on the first day of the battle and ______ taken prisoner or wounded.

2. Look at sources F and G, as well as the text. Why did the artillery not destroy the wire?

3. From sources D and E, explain why most German soldiers were safe during the bombardment.

TANKS AT THE SOMME AND CAMBRAI

The artillery failed miserably at the Battle of the Somme but another weapon, used in far fewer numbers and with far less expectation of success, performed outstandingly well. A handful of tanks were used for the first time in battle in September 1916 during the Battle of the Somme. Their appearance was as much a surprise to the British as it was to the Germans.

H Something was brought near to the Reserve Trench, camouflaged with a big sheet . . . we were at the parapet waiting to go over and waiting for the tank. We heard this chunk, chunk, chunk . . . the Germans ran for their lives, couldn't make out what was firing at them. We didn't know about tanks, they didn't know about tanks but the tank just carried on, knocking down walls and houses.

Pt C Cole (Coldstream Guards)

The Germans called the tanks 'Devil's coaches'. They were the ideal weapon for trench warfare – they flattened the wire and machine gun bullets bounced off them. Only a direct hit from a shell could destroy them, but there were other faults. They were uncomfortable for a start:

J There is not one of us who will ever forget his first ride in a tank. We couldn't stand up, the engine roared, we couldn't hear, nor could we see. It was almost completely dark inside.

Sgt Littledale (Tank Corps)

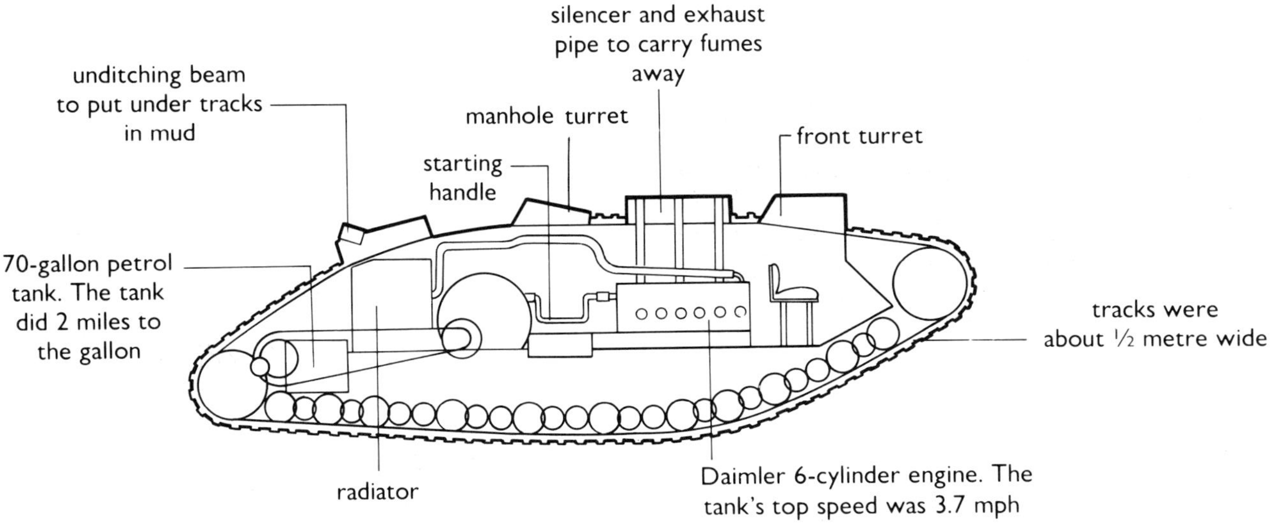

Inside the tank

30 tins food
16 loaves
cheese
tea
sugar
milk

drums engine oil and grease
spare machine gun

4 machine-gun barrels
33,000 rounds ammunition
3 signalling flags
1 lamp signalling set
1 telephone and 90 metres cable
1 basket carrier pigeons + 8 men

I 'A Devil's Coach': specifications.

Often the tanks, which had a top speed of over three miles an hour, broke down or got stuck. In the mud of the Somme or Passchendaele, tanks could get bogged down or simply disappear in giant shell holes. With these conditions, and the lack of spare parts, tanks suffered continual mechanical breakdown and were often held together by the ingenuity of their crews.

K First night: broken fan drive change. Mended it with a nail from a ration box. Second night: broken main drive/flexible coupling. Fitted the spare one. Third night: diff lock jammed in.

Peter Liddle – Testimony of War

The tanks that got through were very effective, however, though the British at the Somme did not have sufficient reserves of men to make the advantage really count. They could not consolidate the gains made by tanks.

To cross trenches, tanks were given bundles of sticks, or fascines. They usually worked in groups of threes, to give each other covering fire while dumping the fascines in the enemy's front line trench and their reserve trench.

L Tank with fascine.

Cambrai

The Somme was not a fair test of the tank. However, it was given a proper test at Cambrai, an area of the German front line made up of firm chalkland. The German defences at Cambrai were formidable, the trenches strongly fortified and the wire fifty metres deep. Tanks advanced after a short barrage and caused panic, as this young German soldier recalled:

M One stared and stared as if one had lost the power of one's limbs. The monsters approached slowly, hobbling, rocking . . . Nothing impeded them; a supernatural force seemed to drive them on. Someone in the trench said the Devil is coming and the word passed along the line like wildfire.

B Cooper – Ironclads at Cambrai

N Tank storming the wire.

At Cambrai the British advanced more than ten kilometres into German territory. At Amiens in 1918, the tanks were even more successful. Six hundred British and French tanks, supported by aircraft but with no bombardment, stormed through the German lines, pushing the German army into general retreat. Cavalry at last broke out into open countryside for the first time since 1914, but it was an iron horse that had made the breakthrough.

?

1. Looking at the text as well as the sources in this chapter, would you agree that the tank was the ideal weapon for trench warfare? Explain why.
2. Why was Cambrai a fairer test for the tank than the Somme?
3. Imagine you are a German soldier who has just experienced an attack involving a British tank. Either in a diary entry or a letter home, describe your experiences in and feelings during the attack.

12 TOTAL WAR

The government felt that what was going on in Britain was almost as important as winning the war on the Western Front. Indeed, they talked about Britain as the Home Front, suggesting that it was just as much part of the war as the battles in Europe. They decided to keep a very tight control over industry, hours of work, the amount and type of goods produced, wages earned and so on. Strikes were banned and people complaining about their working conditions or pay were often branded as traitors. One worker, in Glasgow during the First World War, commented:

A Longer hours, wage cuts, called a traitor if you tried to get your Union to help . . . I wondered if it was the Germans the Government was fighting, or their own people.

Erl Wilkie – shipyard worker

C A warning for strikers.

B A munitions factory in 1915.

Women at War

Women had wanted to be involved in the war from the start. Patriotic girls felt just as keenly about the war as their brothers or fathers in uniform.

D I wanted to do my bit. My brother was at the Front and what was I doing? Serving at table. What good was that?

May MacDonald

After 1916, the government began to organise women into industry and a variety of other occupations. They had to fill the places of men going into the army and it was also necessary to get workers involved in the production of munitions – shells for the war. New factories were set up and whole new towns built (such as Eastriggs and Gretna in Dumfriesshire) to house the workers and cater for their needs. The work done in munitions factories was always hard and often dangerous – but well paid.

E One munitionette's opinion of war work – 'Munition Wages'

Earning high wages? Yus,
Five quid a week.
A woman, too, mind you,
I calls it dim sweet.

Afraid! Are yer kidding?
With money to spend!
Years back I wore tatters,
Now – silk stockings, mi friend!

I've bracelets and jewellery,
Rings envied by friends;
A sergeant to swank with,
And something to lend.

I drive out in taxis,
Do theatres in style.
And this is mi verdict –
It is jolly worth while.

Rosina Wyatt

A lot of men actually thought that women were not capable of doing the kinds of jobs that men had done before they were called up. They were proved wrong. Women became nurses, bus conductors, train drivers, coalmen, dustmen, farm labourers and even soldiers . . . though they were not, of course, allowed to fight.

"We should miss you, Mary, but your undoubted talent should be offered to the Nation if there is a Woman's Bomb-Dropping Corps."

F *Punch* – 18 August 1915.

In 1918 some women were awarded the vote as a reward for their services in wartime.

?

1 Look at sources A and C. Why were strikers sometimes called traitors?

2 Look at source E. Why did this woman jump at the chance of working in a munitions factory?

3 Look at source F. What attitude does the man in the cartoon have about women working in wartime? How might he have changed this attitude by 1918?

4 Find out which women got the vote in 1918.

THE DEFENCE OF THE REALM ACT

On 8 August 1914, the government passed the Defence of the Realm Act (DORA). It gave the government powers to control what people did and meant that it could pass laws without asking parliament. There were many laws and regulations passed under DORA.

Censorship

It was thought very important for the morale of the people that they did not read the truth about military defeats and disasters. Newspapers were heavily censored, partly to stop the Germans getting vital information about losses, the position of units and so on, and partly to stop the people getting depressed by bad news from the Front. As a result, newspapers twisted the truth, representing defeats as slight setbacks or even, as in the case of the cartoon below, as famous victories.

One journalist commented:

G The Office of Censorship at first permitted us to mention the fact that following a battle the dead on both sides were noticeable. A time came when it only allowed German dead on the battlefield. Later still no dead were permitted.

From Lyn MacDonald – Voices and Images of the Great War

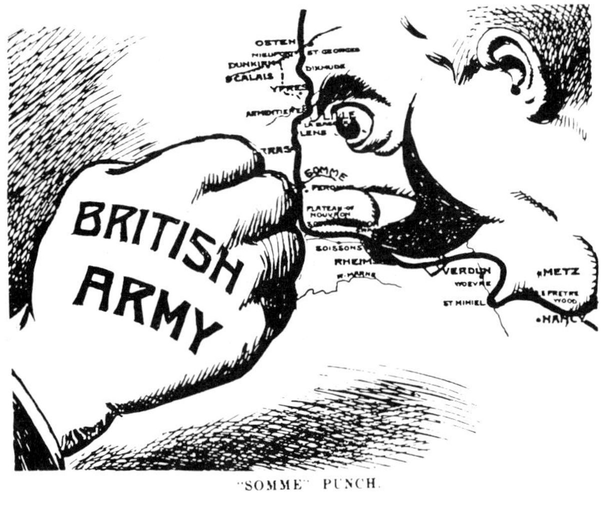

"SOMME" PUNCH.

H *News of the World – 2 July 1916.*

Many people saw the point of censorship, however. In the early months of the war worries about spies seemed more important than accurate newspaper reports, as this letter to *The Times* shows:

I Sir, Is it not possible for the Press of England to take a stand against the spread of false information calculated to play the game of the Germans? The story of the annihilation of two well known regiments a few days ago, and the meeting between Mr Churchill and Lord Kitchener today can only be of use to the Germans.

The Times – 28 August 1914

Alien Registration

Foreign citizens, even people who had lived and worked in Britain for years, were ordered to register as aliens. If they did not do so they could be liable for a substantial fine or even imprisonment. Careful attention was paid to changes of address and even changes of appearance as the extract below shows.

J Humbert Housell, twenty-four, a German hair-dresser, of Church-street, Marylebone, was charged at the same court as a registered alien travelling beyond five miles from his registered address. The prisoner, who was arrested at Leyton, said that he was born in Rome and had a business in Paris. He made application to be a naturalised Frenchman, but, with the war breaking out, his negotiations in that direction had ceased. He produced his registration papers, and his photograph on them showed that he had had his beard removed. Mr Eliot Howard asked why he had shaved off his beard. The prisoner said that he came over from France with the beard, and as he found it was not the custom to wear a beard in England he had shaved it off. He was remanded in custody for enquiries.

Daily Mail – 2 April 1915

Drunkenness

To prevent vital war production suffering from the absenteeism or drunkenness of workers, especially in the important munitions factories, the government passed laws controlling the hours of opening in public bars. In some places, women, who were thought to be even more in danger of succumbing to the temptations of strong drink, were not even allowed out of doors after a certain time at night.

THE ENEMY'S ALLY.

K The evils of drink – Cartoon in *Punch*.

Conscription

The government also passed a law, the first of its type ever in British history, making it compulsory for fit men of a certain age to join the army. This was called the National Service Act. It came about simply because the level of volunteers after 1915 could not keep pace with the frighteningly high level of casualties on the Western Front. People understandably were no longer as keen to enlist as they had been in 1914, as this extract shows:

L Excellent as the recruiting returns are, the need is vital and immediate for more men. There has been an overwhelming difficulty in making many eligible men understand that their services are vitally required.

The Times – May 1916

MILITARY SERVICE ACT
1916

EVERY UNMARRIED MAN
of
MILITARY AGE
Not excepted or exempted under this Act
CAN CHOOSE
ONE OF TWO COURSES:

(1) He can ENLIST AT ONCE and join the Colours without delay:
(2) He can ATTEST AT ONCE UNDER THE GROUP SYSTEM and be called up in due course with his Group.

If he does neither, a third course awaits him.
HE WILL BE DEEMED TO HAVE ENLISTED
under the Military Services Act
ON THURSDAY, MARCH 2ND 1916.
HE WILL BE PLACED IN THE RESERVE AND BE CALLED UP IN HIS CLASS.
as the Military Authorities may determine.

M The Military Service Act.

?

1. Look at the sources and the text. Why was it necessary for the government to pass the Defence of the Realm Act?
2. Look at sources G and H and the text. Why must you be careful when basing your views of events in the war on newspaper reports?
3. Look at sources G, H, I and the text. Think of the arguments for and against censorship in wartime. Turn this into a role play exercise, with one person strongly in favour of censorship and the other against.
4. Look at all the sources. Do you think DORA was a popular Act? Explain your opinion.

13 THE RAZOR AND THE NOOSE

THE RAZOR

In 1917 the German government took a desperate gamble to try to knock Britain out of the war. In a note to the Kaiser, the German naval chiefs thought that they could:

A . . . wound England most seriously by injuring her trade. By means of the U-boat we should be able to inflict the greatest injury.

Note from the German navy to the Kaiser (1917)

B A German submarine at work.

By 1917, Germany had 105 U-boats and the Kaiser was assured by the Chief of the Naval Staff that he could force Britain to its knees before the summer harvest. He was also convinced that America would either not enter the war, or have no influence even if it did. This was to be a fatal mistake.

In February 1917 the Germans began their submarine campaign which was to attack any ships approaching Britain. The campaign was so successful that one ship in four was sunk by the U-boats.

Food supplies in Britain

Since 1914 the U-boats had been an increasing menace, but in 1917 shortages in sugar, margarine, milk, tea, butter, bacon and pork – as well as in other foodstuffs – became critical. Some types of food were so scarce that people were prepared to fight for them.

C At Wrexham a wagon laden with potatoes was surrounded by hundreds of people, chiefly women, who scrambled on to the vehicle. Several women fainted in the struggle and the police were sent for to restore order.

Observer – 8 April 1917

The danger to Britain was so great that the government was forced to act. In December 1916, David Lloyd George became Prime Minister and he took steps to maintain food supplies.

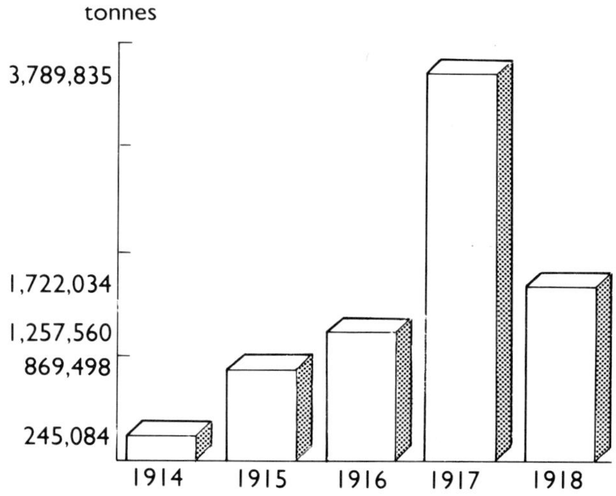

D The rising threat from U-boats – The chart shows the tonnage of British shipping lost in each year of the war.

Rationing

To begin with, people were asked to limit the amount of bread, meat and sugar which they ate each week – a voluntary rationing scheme. However, as the shortages became worse in 1917, the government had to bring in a proper scheme of rationing to try to ensure that everyone got a fair share of certain basic foodstuffs – sugar, meat, butter and margarine and bacon and ham. Even so, the price of bread rose sharply. This affected the poor more than the rich.

RATIONED ITEMS	UNRATIONED ITEMS use with care	UNRATIONED ITEMS use freely no limit
SUGAR	TEA	EGGS
MEAT	MILK	POTATOES
BUTTER AND MARGARINE	JAM	FRUIT
BACON AND HAM	OATMEAL, RICE ETC.	FISH
	BREAD AND CHEESE	VEGETABLES
	BOTTLED FRUITS	

E Food was never in such short supply that Britons had to starve. However, some items were rationed as the table shows.

Propaganda

The government began a poster campaign asking the British people to help beat the U-boats and, to increase food supplies, more land was planted. For instance, public parks were often given over to potatoes and people were asked to grow more of their own food.

F The British people were asked to avoid waste in 1917 as one out of every four ships sailing out of British ports was being sunk by U-boats.

Convoys

Meanwhile, Lloyd George insisted that the convoy system should be used at sea to protect British ships. Within weeks, it was shown to be a great success. Germany had just missed slashing Britain's jugular vein, but, at the same time, the Allied blockade was hurting Germany – like a noose slowly strangling the country.

?

1. What caused the food shortages in Britain in 1917?
2. What evidence is there that the U-boats were successful in 1917?
3. Identify five ways used by the British government to beat the threat of the U-boats.
4. Of what is source F an example?
5. **Investigation:** Find out about new forms of technology which were introduced to defeat the U-boats at sea.

THE NOOSE

Before 1914 the French and British had agreed that Britain's navy would immediately enforce a blockade of German ports on the outbreak of war to prevent supplies reaching Germany. As long as they believed that the war would be 'over by Christmas', the threat of a British blockade did not worry the Germans. The war, though, was not over by Christmas and, by 1917, food and essential industrial raw materials were in short supply. To make matters worse, the harvest of 1916 failed and the winter of 1916–17 became known as the 'turnip winter' as the German people were forced to eat animal fodder to survive. The effect of the food shortages is described by Lilo Linke, who, as a young girl, experienced the shortages at first hand.

G Soon after the outbreak of war the food shortage began. Day after day we had to queue up for the barest necessities of life. My mother never ate her full rations but went without in order to feed Fritz and me a little better than our tiny share would have allowed her.

Lilo Linke – The Great War, I was there

Rationing had been introduced in Germany in 1915 but, by 1917, housewives found that supplies often ran out before they reached the head of the queue and so, to overcome the desperate shortages, the Germans began to produce substitutes (*ersatz*), but these were often foul tasting and seldom healthy. Lilo Linke recalled:

H A soup kitchen in Berlin showing the extent of the food shortages in Germany.

I For days we nourished ourselves on a sweet, greenish pulp; indigestible ruins of frozen potatoes – or perhaps they were only imitations like the rest of our food. Sand was the essential ingredient of a certain type of soup and of a 'sand'-wich paste. Sand I heard scratch under the spoon on my plate, sand I saw in tiny clods on my potatoes, sand I felt between my teeth.

Lilo Linke

J In Berlin, public parks were used for growing food since it was in such short supply.

By 1917, each man was rationed to a quarter of a loaf per day and a tiny amount of butter and, in that year, Germans ate only a quarter of the amount of meat they had eaten in 1914. Millions of Germans were seriously underfed and an English woman who was married to a German and so lived in Berlin during the war said:

K . . . We are growing thinner every day . . . we are gaunt and bony now. Our thoughts are taken up with wondering what our next meal will be.

Weakness brought about by lack of nourishment made the Germans more open to disease and, when Spanish Flu struck Germany at the end of the war, perhaps as many as one million died because they were unable to fight it.

The Collapse of German Morale

L The arrival of the Americans and their industrial power meant the end for German hopes of winning the war.

M American soldiers leaving for Europe

1917	October	38,000
	November	23,000
	December	49,000
1918	January	46,000
	February	48,000
	March	84,000
	April	117,000
	May	244,000
	June	276,000

The strains of economic strangulation began to show in 1917. America had entered the war in April as a result of the unrestricted U-boat campaign and this had a devastating effect on German morale. Unrest grew and strikes spread as many Germans came to see that their case was now hopeless.

N The food situation is unbearable. The bread ration was reduced this spring. The potato supply has been insufficient. During the past month labourers had to live on dry bread and a little meat. Undernourishment is spreading. Conditions making for health are impaired. When we face this situation, we have to say 'our strength is almost spent'.

Friedrich Ebert (July 1917) – German politician

German industry also suffered shortages, especially of fuel and chemicals for munitions. In one of the strange ironies of the war, German soldiers who were part of Ludendorff's successful offensive of 1918 were dismayed to discover that the Allies could afford to abandon large quantities of brass, rubber, and copper as well as guns and shells. With American industrial might behind them the British and the French would never run out of essential supplies. General Fuller of the British army said this of the German soldier:

O Wedged between his starving family and a hopeless future, his morale was shattered by the realisation that the succession of offensives since 21 March had been in vain.

General Fuller

The German soldiers realised that they could remain on the defensive, but they would not now win the war. The Ludendorff Offensive was halted in April 1918 and the tide of battle once more swung in favour of the Allies. The noose which had been slowly strangling Germany finally closed in November 1918 when the Germans accepted the terms of an armistice and on 11 November at 11 o'clock in the morning, the war to end all wars came to a silent conclusion.

?

1. Using evidence from the sources describe the effects of the blockade on German civilians during the First World War.
2. Why are sources G, I, K and N valuable to a historian studying the effects of the blockade in Germany?
3. How important was (a) the blockade and (b) the entry of America in bringing about Germany's defeat in 1918?

14 PUNISHMENT OF THE GUILTY

President Wilson of America arrived in Europe in January 1919 as the leading figure at the Peace Conference. He came with a Fourteen Point Programme on which the peace was to be based, but his ideas differed greatly from those of Lloyd George and Clemenceau (the French Prime Minister). Wilson wanted a peace in which Germany would not be punished. Clemenceau wanted to destroy Germany in order to protect France. Lloyd George did not want as harsh a peace settlement as Clemenceau, but they all had to take account of what people wanted.

Public opinion

Public opinion in Britain and France was not yet ready to accept the kind of peace which Wilson suggested. Rudyard Kipling spoke for the ordinary people of both countries when he wrote:

A These were our children who died for our lands: they were dear in our sight. We have only the memory left of their home-treasured sayings and laughter. The price of our loss shall be paid to our hands, not another's hereafter.

Rudyard Kipling – The Honours of War

The British and French had suffered too much – too many dead, wounded, maimed and disfigured soldiers; too much destruction on land and at sea – and the time was not yet right for forgiving. 'The price of our loss shall be paid to our hands' – with these words Kipling said what many felt – those who had been responsible for starting the war should be made to pay for it.

B The attitudes of the peacemakers towards Germany and the Peace.

THE COST OF THE WAR

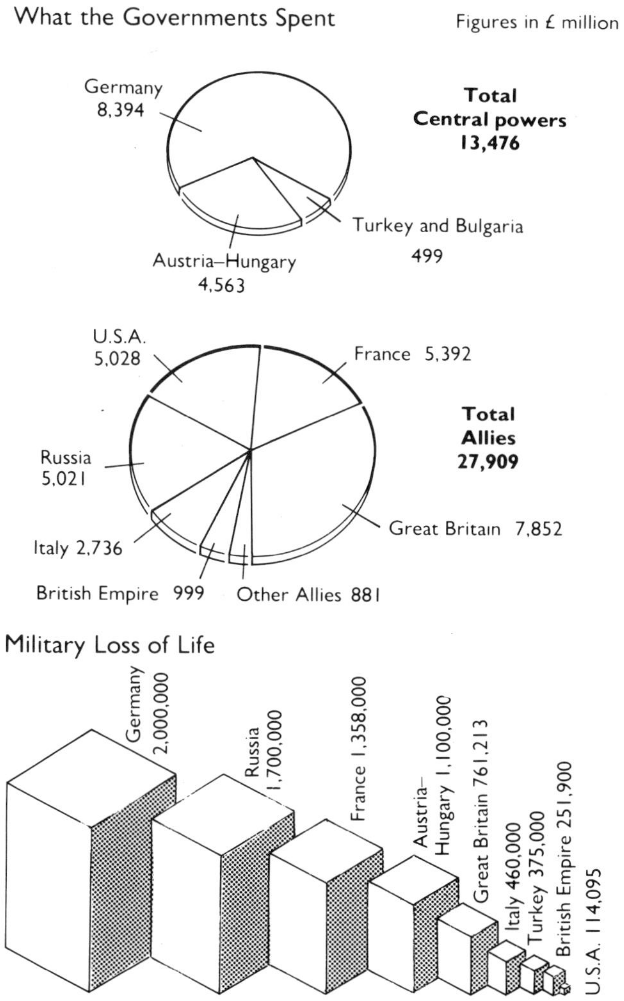

C The cost of the war

● *War Guilt*

The war had caused a huge amount of damage which had to be repaired. As the war ended, the victor powers began to discuss the question 'who should pay?' The solution seemed simple – Germany had invaded Belgium and France and so should pay compensation. This would have pleased the Belgians and French – but it did not take account of how much the war had cost Britain and the Empire. It was necessary to write a clause into the Treaty which made it clear that the war had been caused by the Germans. This is what the Treaty of Versailles said:

D Germany accepts responsibility for causing all the loss and damage to which the Allied governments have been subjected as a consequence of the war imposed upon them by the aggression of Germany and her allies.

Treaty of Versailles (1919)

There was no doubt that certain individuals had been responsible for actions which had led to the war. However, no strong attempt was made to put the Kaiser on trial, nor was any other individual blamed. Instead, responsibility was placed on the German nation – because the nation could be forced to repay what the victorious powers thought was their due. In London, the people were promised that:

E We shall squeeze the German lemon till the pips squeak.

Sir Arthur Geddes

Even Lloyd George was eventually heard to remark:

F The Germans must pay to their last farthing and we shall search their pockets for it.

David Lloyd George

The 'guilty' were about to be punished.

?

1. What word best describes the type of peace wanted by (a) Clemenceau and (b) Wilson? How did Lloyd George's attitude change?
2. Why were Clemenceau's ideas more acceptable to ordinary people? (Use sources B and C.)
3. Why was Germany to be punished?
4. **Discussion:** Was it fair to blame the German nation for having caused the war? (Refer to Chapter 7.)

THE TREATY OF VERSAILLES

Clemenceau's victory

At the Peace Talks, Wilson and Lloyd George had urged moderation as they did not wish to leave Germany with a desire for revenge. However, between January and May 1919, the tide swung against them and in favour of Clemenceau.

Wilson's decline

The change in leadership at the Conference happened for three main reasons. Firstly, an attempted assassination of Clemenceau gained the old Prime Minister a great deal of sympathy.

G In an instant, Clemenceau had replaced Wilson as the hero of the conference. Having shot Clemenceau, the assassin had wounded Wilson.

Charles Mee – The End of Old Order

Secondly, Wilson's views of American involvement in world affairs were not shared by all of his fellow countrymen. At home his party lost control of the Senate and, from then onwards, he no longer spoke for all America. The American Congress eventually refused to sign, thus isolating America from Europe and from the new League of Nations. Thirdly, public opinion in 1919 would not have accepted a peace which was not seen to limit German power.

When the German delegation was ordered to the Hall of Mirrors in the Palace of Versailles, they were presented with a dictated Peace based much more on the views of Clemenceau than had been originally expected.

PEACE TREATY FOR GERMANY
STERN BUT JUST
THE ALLIES' TERMS

FRENCH FRONTIER OF 1870 RESTORED

£5,000,000,000 INDEMNITY

ALLIED TROOPS ON RHINE FOR FIFTEEN YEARS

Terms Presented – The Germans were presented with the Allied Peace Treaty at Versailles yesterday afternoon. The sitting did not last an hour, and the time was occupied with the speech of M.Clemenceau, in handing over the Treaty to the enemy delegation, and with Count Brockdorff-Rantzau's reply.

"The time has come when we must settle our accounts," said M.Clemenceau, adding that the Germans had asked for peace, and the Allies were ready to give it. But, he added, the Second Treaty of Versailles had been bought at too great a price to allow the Allies to do other than guard themselves against a recrudescence of another war.

Count Rantzau, in reply, repudiated the suggestion that the entire responsibility for the war rested on Germany's shoulders, and asserted that Germany alone had not been guilty of atrocities.

£5,000,000,000 – By the terms of the Treaty, for the consideration of which fifteen days are allowed, Germany is made responsible for indemnities amounting to £5,000,000,000. £1,000,000,000 is due within two years, and bonds to the amount of £4,000,000,000 are to be held by the Allies.

Back to France – The French frontier of 1870 is restored, with a reservation regarding the Saar Valley. The restoration of Alsace-Lorraine to France is described as dating from the signing of the Armistice. In return for her ruined mines, France receives the full ownership of the mines in the Saar Valley.

Belgium and Poland – A section of Prussian territory is to be ceded to Belgium. To Poland must be given Upper Silesia, Posen, and part of the province of West Prussia. Danzig is to be a free city under the League of Nations.

New German Army – Germany's new Army must not exceed 100,000 men, including not more than 4000 officers. No reserve of officers with war experience will be permitted. Armament production must be limited in accordance with the size of the army.

Rhine Occupation – To guarantee the execution of the Treaty, German territory to the west of the Rhine, together with the bridgeheads, will be occupied by Allied forces for 15 years. If, before the expiration of 15 years, Germany complies with all the Treaty undertakings, the occupying troops will be withdrawn immediately.

H This appeared in the Scottish newspaper, the *Daily Record*, on 8 May 1919.

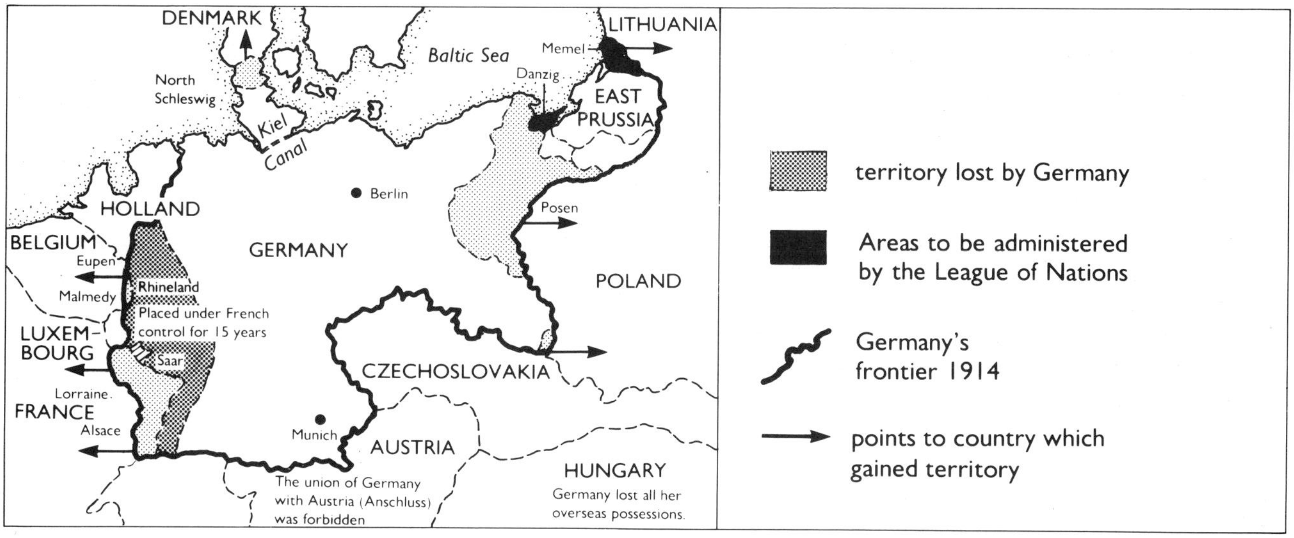

I German territorial losses at Versailles.

Repercussions of the Peace

The German delegation to Versailles made the following statement which was also reported on the *Daily Record's* front page on 8 May 1919:

J THE GERMAN REPLY
SPIRITED REPUDIATION OF BLOOD-GUILTINESS

It is demanded of us that we shall confess ourselves to be the only ones guilty of the war. Such a confession in my mouth would be a lie. The German Government's action and omissions in the tragic twelve days of July certainly contributed to the disaster, but we energetically deny that Germany and its people, who were convinced that they were making a war of defence, were alone guilty.

Count Brockdorff-Rantzeau – Daily Record 8 May 1919

The victor powers were not impressed by the German protests and on 28 June 1919, the German delegation was summoned to the Hall of Mirrors to sign the Peace Treaty. German public opinion was outraged at the humiliation of Versailles and, that day, the *Deutsche Zeitung* printed as its leading story this call to the German nation

K VENGEANCE! GERMAN NATION!

Today in the Hall of Mirrors a disgraceful Treaty is being signed. Never forget it! On the spot where, in the glorious year of 1871, the German Empire in all its glory began, today German honour is dragged to the grave. Never forget it! The German people, with unceasing labour, will push forward to reconquer that place among the nations of the world to which they are entitled. There will be a vengeance for the shame of 1919.

Deutsche Zeitung – 28 June 1919

?

1. Discuss why Wilson, Clemenceau and Lloyd-George had such different views on how Germany should be dealt with after the war.
2. Describe the changing roles of Wilson and Clemenceau at the Peace Conference of 1919.
3. Explain why Wilson lost control of the Conference. Use source G.
4. Summarise the main terms of the Treaty under the following headings by using sources H and I. (a) war guilt and reparations; (b) territorial; (c) military.
5. How did the Germans react to the accusation of War Guilt? (Source J.)
6. Compare the *Daily Record* (H) and the *Deutsche Zeitung* (K):
   (a) 'Stern but just' – To what extent does the German newspaper agree with this statement?
   (b) Why should historians studying Versailles be cautious when using sources like these newspaper articles?

15 THE LEAGUE OF NATIONS

RECONSTRUCTION: A NEW YEAR'S TASK

A Rebuilding the world – the view from *Punch* (1919).

There had been many wars in the history of the world, but none had the impact in suffering of the Great War. So terrible had it been that it convinced many people that the end of the First World War would be the end of all war.

The American President, Woodrow Wilson, was determined to build into the Treaty of Versailles a system to preserve peace and security in the world so that no country would ever want or need to go to war again. He passionately believed that some real good could emerge from the chaos and disaster of the war. In London he said:

B Many terrible things have come out of this war, gentlemen, but some very beautiful things have come out of it. Wrong has been defeated . . . people that were suspicious of one another can now live as friends . . . in a single family . . . distrust . . . is cleared away. We are brothers and have a common goal.

Woodrow Wilson

In his Fourteen Point Plan Wilson said that an international organisation was needed to prevent wars. The idea of a league of nations was not a new one, but Wilson was determined to make it part of the Peace Treaty at Versailles, so that countries could not say they agreed with it and then try to wriggle out of their promises later on.

The League, as Wilson saw it, had two simple tasks: to keep the peace and to make the world a better place to live in. The final form (or Covenant) of the League of Nations was agreed on 13 February 1919. The Covenant promised:

C Should any country resort to war . . . it shall be the duty of the council . . . to recommend what force shall be used to protect the Covenant of the League.

Article 16, League Covenant

The League was not just designed to provide security, but also to improve the well-being of people by getting rid of some of the long-lasting problems that had haunted them for centuries, like slavery, ill health, poor housing.

LEAGUE OF NATIONS

QUESTION OF SLAVERY

COMMUNICATION FROM THE GOVERNMENT OF THE SUDAN

Note by the Secretary-General:

The Secretary-General has the honour to circulate for the information of the Council and the Members of the League the following letter from the Government of the Sudan regarding the question of slavery.

D Other aspects of the League of Nations (1).

SPECIAL DEPARTMENTS

Health:	to work on improving the health of all the people of the world
Drugs:	to advise people on the dangers of drugs and try to stop illegal trading
Refugees:	to help the refugees of wars and natural disasters to survive and rebuild their lives
Leprosy:	to help lepers and to find ways of wiping out this disease
Slavery:	to find out where slavery still existed in the world and campaign for it to be ended

E Other aspects of the League of Nations (2).

The Organisation of the League

The League had an Assembly – a kind of parliament – of all the member states which met once a year. It was governed by a Council of major powers, including Britain and France, which took the important decisions, and aided by a Secretariat which took care of all the administration. There was an international Court of Justice to sort out legal problems and a series of committees were set up to investigate matters of health, work, housing and so on.

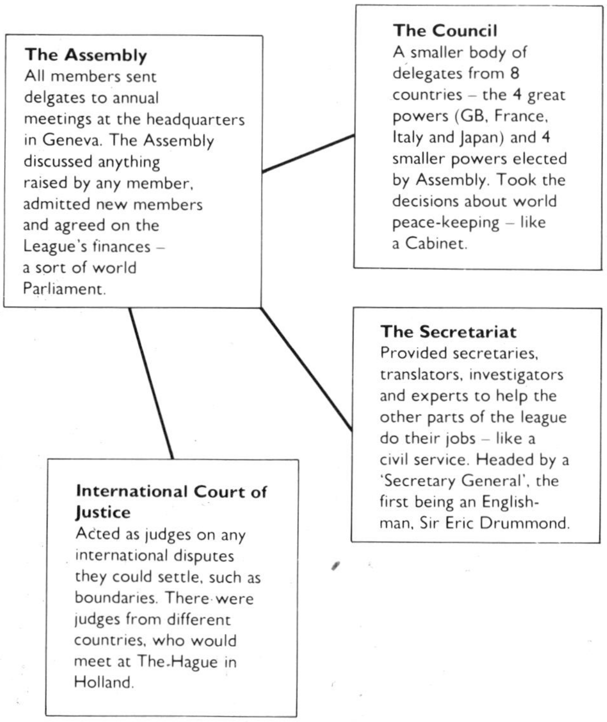

F The structure of the League.

Although the League had plenty of critics, it was enthusiastically supported by people in Europe.

G A League of Nations Rally (1921).

?

1 Copy and complete the table below:

Body	**Composition/Role**
Council	Consisted of ________ powers.
	Took all the major ________.
Assembly	Consisted of all the ________.
	Held meetings every ________.
________	Took care of all the administration.
Court of ________	Sorted out ________ problems.

2 Think about everything you have studied so far. Why do you think so many people in Europe were enthusiastic about the League?

FRANCE AND SECURITY

The French attitude to the League of Nations was very different from that shown by the USA and Wilson. Their point of view was simple. They believed that their security was very important and that the best way to ensure this security was to crush the Germans so they could never threaten France again. This was an understandable attitude for a country involved in two devastating wars against the Germans in the space of fifty years. Clemenceau, the tough little French Prime Minister, was suspicious of Wilson and suspicious of the League. As he said:

H How can I talk to a fellow who thinks himself the first man for 2000 years who has known anything about peace on earth . . .? Wilson has fourteen points but God only had ten.

G. Clemenceau (1919)

At the Versailles discussions, it soon became clear that the French were determined to pursue their simple objective: revenge against the Germans with an assurance that Germany would never again be in a strong enough position to threaten European peace. This meant a weak Germany but a strong France – an idea opposed by Wilson, who believed in general disarmament among nations. The French aim was to keep their weapons in readiness. Clemenceau said to Wilson:

I If I accepted what you propose for the security of France after the millions who had died and the millions who have suffered . . . I hope that my successor would have me shot.

G. Clemenceau (1919)

If there had to be a League of Nations, Clemenceau wanted it to have a large standing army commanded by French generals and wanted it to exclude Germany. This would make it an old style Alliance aimed at Germany with French security guaranteed by Britain and the USA.

Clemenceau was forced to compromise on the League in order to achieve his more important objectives of weakening Germany. The League did not bind itself to having a standing army or even to backing up its decisions with the threat of force, though it did, on French insistence, exclude Germany. The French, therefore, decided to form its own system of alliances designed to encircle Germany, and France also maintained a great disrespect for the League.

J The French alliances.

K Alliances signed by the French in the 1920s

1920 Belgium
1921 Poland
1924 Czechoslovakia
1925 Locarno Pact (guaranteed French borders)
1926 Romania
1927 Yugoslavia

GERMANY AND SECURITY

By the terms of the Treaty of Versailles, Germany had been disarmed and the French policy of encirclement left it feeling vulnerable and isolated. The countries on Germany's eastern borders, Poland and Czechoslovakia, also maintained very large armed forces and this increased German fears of invasion.

L The French are determined to keep us naked and alone. In such a situation we must look new places for friends.

Count Von Brockdorff

In 1923 the French invaded the Ruhr and, the year after, Gustav Stresseman, the German Foreign Minister, decided on a twin course of action: to press for Germany's acceptance into the League and to search elsewhere for allies. He believed that he could achieve changes to the worst parts of the Versailles Treaty by working closely with Britain and France inside the League.

M All the questions close to German hearts – war guilt, disarmament, the Saarland etc – are matters for the League and a skilful speaker might make them disagreeable for the Entente.

Gustav Stresemann

N Gustav Stresemann, the most influential German politician 1924-29.

Germany also signed the Treaty of Rapallo with Russia, another European outcast since 1917, promising mutual co-operation in economic and even military matters.

OVERWEIGHTED

PRESIDENT WILSON: "Here's your olive branch. Now get busy."
DOVE OF PEACE: "Of course, I want to please everybody, but isn't this a bit thick?"

O One view of the League – a *Punch* cartoon (1919).

?

1. From the text and the sources describe and explain France's attitude to the League of Nations.
2. **Role Play:** Taking the parts of the French and the Americans, imagine the kind of arguments used at Versailles over the role of the League of Nations and act these out, or write a small one act play.
3. What additional steps did France take to ensure her security outside the League in the 1920s?
4. Describe how Stresemann planned to change Britain's and France's minds on issues like the Saarland.
5. Look at source O. Who do you think thought the League a bit 'too thick'? Why?

16 THE STANDARD OF LIVING IN GERMANY

At the end of the First World War, the German people were starving. The British blockade on German ports had stopped food coming into the country, and the harvests failed too, making the situation even worse. Thousands starved, or were struck down by epidemics such as influenza.

A We have got through . . . the worst week the German people has had to face up to. No coal, electric light turned off, gas turned down and practically no food – there seems to be no more potatoes . . . we have been given peelings.

Quoted in J Brooman –
Twentieth Century History

By 1918, the average adult German was living on 1000 calories a day, about half the amount needed for healthy living. Coal was running out and, since electric power and gas depended on coal, there were frequent power cuts. In cities, all places of entertainment, cinemas, restaurants and bars were shut. Lights in private houses were put off in the early evening.

B German housewives queue for potato peelings.

● *Inflation*

In the Treaty of Versailles, Germany was made to pay reparations. The new German government paid the first installment but could not pay the second. The French army invaded the Ruhr in 1923 in retaliation and the workers in the Ruhr went on strike. Since the Ruhr was one of Germany's most important industrial centres, this made the German economy even weaker. To get over the crisis, the government printed more paper money, but this caused prices to rise quickly. This was called inflation and in Germany it was so bad they called it hyperinflation. It meant that wages bought nothing, as this German explained:

C As soon as I received my salary I rushed out to buy the necessities. My daily salary as an editor was just enough to buy a loaf of bread and a small piece of cheese . . . I had to refuse to go on a lecture to the other side of town because I wasn't sure the fee would cover my train fare.

Frieda Wunderlich

Wages could not keep pace with prices even though workers were paid twice daily and threw the wads of notes out of the window to members of their families who would rush to buy things before the prices went up again!

D A German banknote, with new value stamped on top.

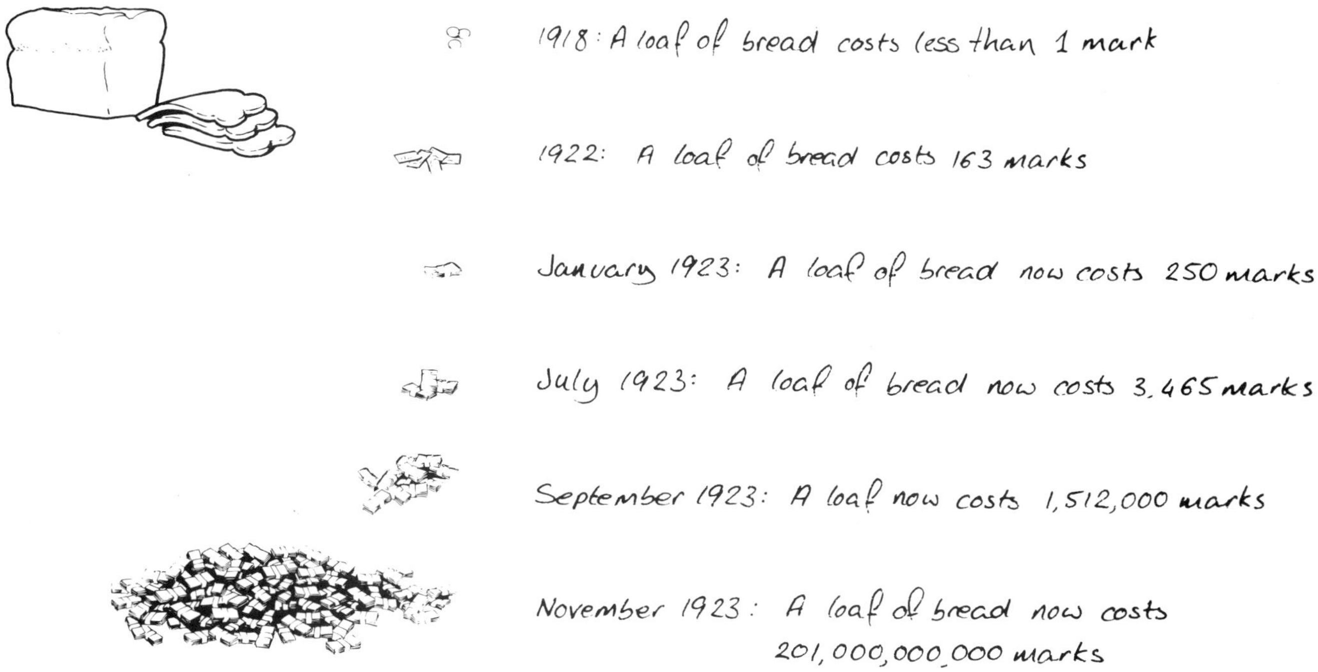

E Inflation 1918–23.

F An acquaintance came in from the suburbs with his monthly salary to buy a pair of shoes for his baby. By the time he got here he could only buy a cup of coffee.

Frieda Wunderlich

The scrap value of the banknotes, weighed by a scrap paper merchant, could actually get a worker more goods than trying to use the money in the shops. Everyone suffered. Savings were wiped out. Women, children, unemployed men, ex-soldiers, had to resort to begging in the streets or scavenging for scraps. Production throughout the whole of Germany slumped, sending even more people out of work.

G An ex-officer begs in the street.

?

1. Using the sources and the text complete the following paragraph:

   At Versailles Germany was forced to pay ________. When they couldn't make the payments, the French invaded the ________, one of the richest parts of Germany. The workers went on ________. To solve the crisis the government printed more ________. Wages, however, couldn't keep pace and many people were forced to ________ in the streets.

2. Look at sources A and B. Why were German women prepared to queue for potato peelings?
3. Look at sources C and F. What problems did hyperinflation cause for people on a salary?
4. Look at source G. How useful a source is this for understanding the standard of living in Germany after 1918?

EFFECTS OF THE WAR ON LIVING STANDARDS IN BRITAIN

H People said when we enlisted,
Fame and medals we should win,
But the fame is in the Guard Room,
And the medals made of tin.
Now we've finished with the Kaiser,
At the Empire we shall sing
The Battalion National Anthem
Twice a night. God Save the King!

Soldier's Poem (1919)

After the long and terrible years of war, few of the men wanted or expected a hero's welcome. A lot of things had happened since the enthusiastic days of August 1914 and most people wanted to try as much as they could to forget about the war and to live ordinary lives again. There had been little celebration, even, at the news of the Armistice which was greeted with a kind of glum relief, but no real emotion. As one old soldier commented:

I At 11am the village bell rang. On our side there were only a few shouts. I had heard more for a rum ration. The match was over and it had been a damned bad game.

Colonel Nicholson (Suffolk Regiment)

J Saviours of Civilisation – Old soldiers selling matches.

Many of the soldiers, being demobbed after the war, could expect little peace of mind. It *had* been a damned bad game and many ex-soldiers were to be mentally scarred by their experiences.

K Us fellows, it took us years to get over it. Years. Long afterwards, when you were working, married, had kids . . . you'd see it all before you. Many's the time I got up and tramped the streets until daybreak . . . and many's the time I'd meet other fellows out there doing the same thing.

Rifleman F White (King's Royal Rifles)

Robert Graves remembers:

L . . . shells bursting on my bed at midnight, strangers would assume the faces of men who had been killed.

Robert Graves – Goodbye to All That

Little peace could be expected for the veterans of the Great War, but they did expect something. After having sacrificed so much for their country, they believed they had earned the basic right to make a living after the war and bring up their families in reasonable prosperity. They had often been reminded in the trenches of how grateful the country was to them for their efforts. Now they wanted some return, in the shape of a job, a house and enough money to buy a few luxuries. They were disappointed. Newspapers, in the first years after the war, were filled with little adverts like these:

M Situations vacant (1920)

COMMANDER, RN retired, aged 44, married, shortly demobilised, exceptional experience, executive officer of ships for many years, 2 years in command, total abstainer. WANTS WORK. Moderate salary.

OFFICER, well educated, capable organiser and administrator, wide secretarial experience, keen, energetic, tactful, good horseman, experienced athlete, desires post as secretary or secretary-manager, home or abroad; excellent references.

After the war, many people had expected the economy to expand as trade began to grow again between the countries of the world, creating greater prosperity, more jobs and so on. This had not happened. An economic depression followed the war and even people who had been in secure employment during the war found themselves out in the cold as factories shut or cut back their workforce. Soldiers coming back from Europe found the situation impossible. There were no jobs, no houses.

N I had to walk round and took a seat on the embankment. I must have dozed off . . . I woke and what a sight it was. All the seats were full of old soldiers in all sorts of dress but mostly khaki – and a few more were lying on the steps, some wrapped up in old newspapers.

Trooper S Chaplin (Northants Yeomanry)

Some counted themselves lucky to be put up in old railway carriages with no running water, and to get odd jobs, street cleaning or as messenger boys. It was a terrible humiliation for men who, a few months previously, had been hailed as saviours of their country. Many were enraged. So were women, who, having been enlisted to do all sorts of jobs after 1916, were immediately made unemployed when the men came home.

P Only a few months before they had been hailed as patriots . . . but now they were vampires who deprived men of their rightful jobs.

R Graves and A Hodge – The Long Weekend

Horror at the war and disillusionment about life after it led many to question the reasons they had fought at all. Certainly they began to question whether they should continue to support the kind of people who had sent them off to war but who had then been unable to provide them a dignified living when they came home.

O Labour Party posters – the simple truth for many ex-soldiers.

?

1. Why did the soldier in source I think it had been 'a damned bad game'?
2. What was the experience of many soldiers who came home from the front expecting a job and a decent standard of living?
3. What is being shown in source J?
4. Look at the two posters shown in source O. What is their message? How far is this propaganda?
5. Look at source H. What do you think the writer means by 'medals made of tin'?

17 DISARMAMENT IN THE 1920s

A Poison

Forget, and forgive them – you say
War's bitterness passes;
Wild rose wreaths the gun-pit today,
Where the trench was, young grass is;
Forget and forgive:
Let them live.

Gilbert Frankau

Disarmament had always been one of the main parts of President Wilson's plan for the new post-war world. It had been one of his fourteen points:

B National armaments will be reduced to the lowest point consistent with domestic safety.

President Woodrow Wilson – Address to Congress, January 1918

The French forced a compromise at Versailles and, as a result, only Germany was disarmed. The other nations had promised to discuss disarmament, however, and through the course of the 1920s several efforts were made to begin real disarmament in the world. There were two main problems, however.

The Problems

1. France

As we saw in Chapter 15, the French were not happy with the League of Nations, the main reason being that they believed it to be toothless. They had argued for the League to have a permanent standing army but this had been rejected. The withdrawal of the USA from European affairs after the Senate rejected the Treaty of Versailles made the French even more frightened. Now they would not have the power of the USA to help them in any war of revenge waged by Germany. The French were still terrified of the Germans, even though Germany had been crippled by the decisions made at Versailles. France believed that Versailles had not been tough enough on the Germans and the last thing the French really wanted to do was disarm. Clemenceau said:

C . . . I am not a pacifist . . . I wage war. In foreign policy I wage war. Always, everywhere, I wage war . . . and I shall continue to wage war till the last quarter hour.

Georges Clemenceau

2. Germany

Germany had been disarmed against its will and this was a cause of great anger in Germany. The invasion of the Ruhr in 1923 showed how powerless Germany was at the hands of the French.

D The French in the Ruhr.

E Signing the Treaty of Locarno.

Under Gustav Stresemann, the Germans began a policy that they hoped might lead to the softening of the Versailles Treaty. This policy of fulfillment meant that Germany reached agreements with Britain and France. These agreements are shown in source G. Secretly, though, Germany was hoping to rearm to defend itself against France.

F Stresemann was an intense nationalist but he saw that Germany's interests might be better served by diplomacy rather than showing one's teeth.

Wiskemann – Europe of the Dictators

The Germans planned to get round the terms of the Versailles Treaty by building aircraft and tanks in other countries such as Russia and Switzerland.

G First steps towards disarmament

1924 Reparations quarrel settled. Attempt begun to put improved relations on a more permanent footing.

1925 Treaty of Locarno settled Germany's western frontier. Unlike Treaty of Versailles, Germany signed voluntarily.

1926 Germany joined the League. Permanent seat on Council.

1928 Kellogg Pact. War renounced as instrument of national policy.

As the 1920s went on, France and Britain seemed better pleased with the attitude of Stresemann and Germany, and several agreements signed between the major powers paved the way for a general conference on disarmament, due to be held in Geneva in 1932.

?

1. Look at the section 'The Problems: 1. France'. What was the French attitude towards (a) German disarmament? (b) French disarmament?
2. Look at source D. Do you think this is a French or German cartoon? Explain your answer. How accurately does this source describe the state of Germany in 1923?
3. Look at source G. Why were the French more willing to talk about disarmament by the end of the 1920s?

PLOUGHSHARES INTO SWORDS

The Collapse of Disarmament

PEACE (sadly): "THIS LOOKS VERY LIKE THE POINT WE STARTED FROM."

H Ten years on.

By 1929, as this cartoon sadly comments, no real progress had been made towards disarmament, although it did seem that the gradual increase of friendship and stability in Europe was a very good sign of things to come. Stresemann had made Germany acceptable again in Europe and, although France was still afraid of a strong Germany, there seemed no danger under Stresemann and his colleagues. Moreover, as explained in Chapter 15, the French had taken their security into their own hands, forming a defensive ring around Germany by a clever arrangement of alliances with the new strong democracies of Eastern Europe. Things looked promising in 1929.

I International goodwill was at a high tide . . . the golden age was at hand.

Mowat – Britain Between the Wars

With international goodwill in this state, the League of Nations set up a committee to make preparations for a Disarmament Conference. It was hoped that all the world's major powers would agree on weapons' reductions to make the world a safer place. However, it took three years to organise the conference and it was February 1932 before the nations met in Geneva. Unfortunately a great deal had happened between 1929 and 1932. Conditions favourable to disarmament had disappeared. By 1932 many of the world's powers had begun to feel a lot less secure.

A Rising Tide of Aggression

The world had become a much more unstable place after 1929.

Italy

Many people thought Mussolini a bit of a clown, but he had striven consistently to improve the economy and the armed strength of Italy to the point where he could claim to challenge Britain and France's dominance of the Mediterranean and North Africa. He did not feel himself bound by international agreements and had said so many times:

J Words are a very fine thing: but rifles, machine guns, warships, aeroplanes and cannons are still finer things – right unaccompanied by might is an empty word.

Benito Mussolini (1929)

Japan

In 1931, using the pretext of a small disturbance on a Japanese controlled railway line, the Japanese had invaded Manchuria. China complained to the League of Nations about the Japanese action. The League sent a group of investigators to Manchuria to find out who was to blame for the trouble. This group took two years to publish their report and, by this time, Manchuria was completely under Japanese control. When Japan ignored the League no action was taken. The League had failed in its first big test as peacemaker.

THE DOORMAT.

K Japan makes a doormat of the League.

Germany

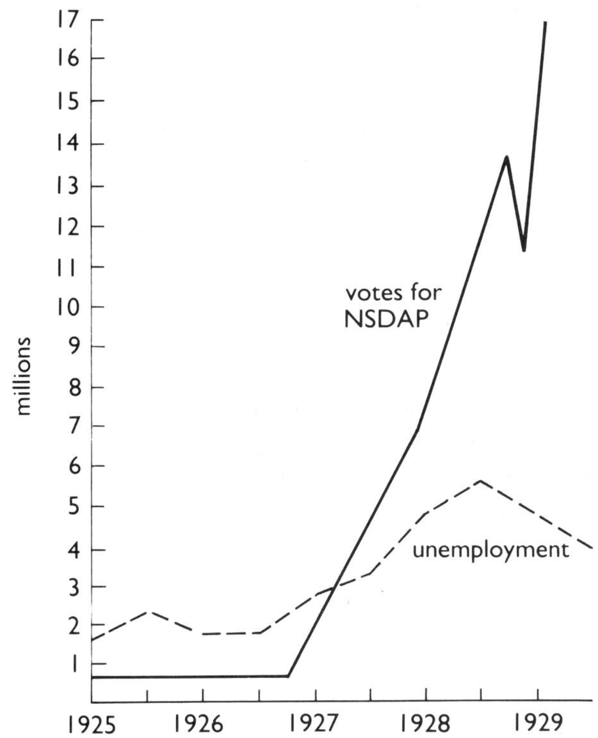

L The rise of the Nazis.

The Nazis, an extreme nationalist party led by Adolf Hitler, had gained many more votes after 1929, and, in 1933, Hitler became Chancellor of Germany. Hitler and the Nazis' views about disarmament and European security were clear.

M We demand the abolition of the Treaty of Versailles . . . we demand land and territory for the nourishment of our people . . . we demand equality in armaments . . .

Programme of the NSDAP

● *Economic Problems*

In 1929, disaster struck the economies of the world with the Wall Street Crash. Banks collapsed. Industries went out of business, savings were wiped out overnight. Inflation and unemployment soared. Many countries bec.me more interested in solving their own econor.ic problems than worrying about the internati.nal events.

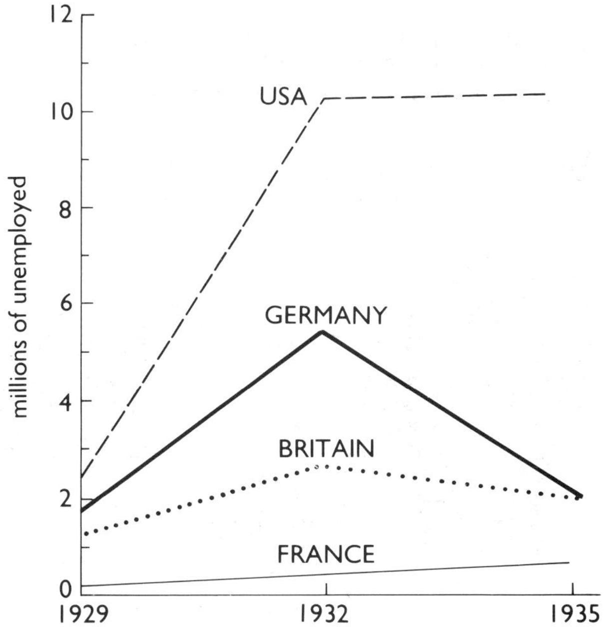

N The depression.

O The two guardians of post war peace, Britain and France, . . . became so preoccupied with their economic problems that they were reluctant to deal with outside problems.

R Stone – The Drift to War

The disarmament conference was a disaster. Germany, under the control of Hitler from half way through the conference, withdrew in 1933. The following year, the conference broke up. Europe gradually abandoned the idea of disarmament and prepared for the worst.

?

1. Why did the time seem right for disarmament in 1929?
2. Look at the text and the sources. Why did the attitude and actions of (a) Italy and (b) Japan make the success of the disarmament conference less likely?
3. Why were disarmament talks less likely to succeed after 1933? Consider France as well as Germany.

18 THE NEW WORLD

The Decline of Britain

A A Ford production line.

As we saw in Chapter 15, the economic depression in Britain meant a period of unemployment and hardship for thousands of people, including ex-soldiers returning from the Western Front. The economy picked up at times during the 1920s but the First World War marked the beginning of the end for Britain as the world's greatest power. She had been overtaken, even as early as 1900.

B Where the power lay.

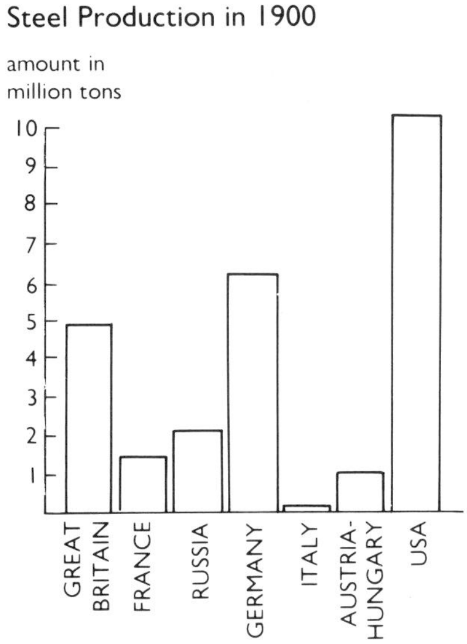

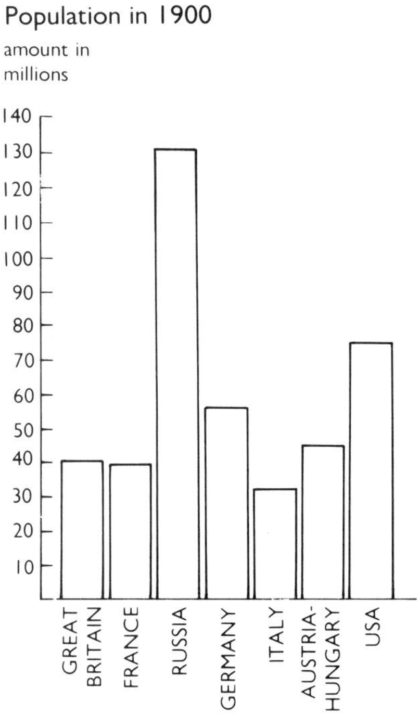

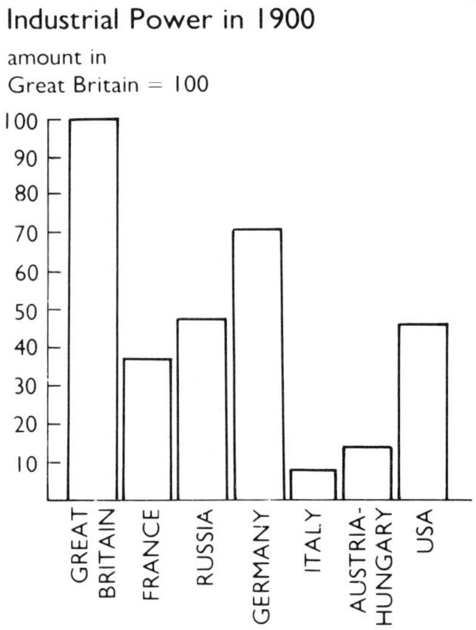

C The United States of America was now a formidable competitor of the old European exporting powers.

AJP Taylor – From Sarajevo to Potsdam

While the European powers had borrowed heavily to pay for the First World War, the USA had actually increased its wealth and Europe was heavily in debt to the USA for very large sums of money. Britain had borrowed 959,000,000 dollars and France 634,000,000 dollars. Moreover, British and French industry had been turned over to war production like munitions rather than making money. Since the USA had entered the war so late, her industry had continued to make wealth and she had picked up trade from parts of the world that used to trade with Britain and France.

Even before the First World War, however, the USA had been outpacing France and Britain.

Lloyd George had looked forward to a period of 'normalcy' in 1919, by which he meant a return to prosperity. What was normal before the war, however, was not to be normal after it. Britain's main sources of wealth, her mining, her shipbuilding and heavy engineering, went into slump. There was a shrinking of trade throughout Europe after the First World War, and countries like the USA and Japan were able to take advantage by capturing markets throughout the world. By 1919, and probably before that time, Britain was no longer the workshop for the rest of the world.

THE DEBTORS

D Debtors – Germany owes France, France owes Britain and Britain owes the USA.

E The decay in coal production.

	1907	*1912*	*1924*
Employment	839,000	980,000	1,183,000
Production	271 m tonnes	265 m tonnes	270 m tonnes
Output per manshift	–	c.950 kg	c.890 kg
Exports	65 m tonnes	65 m tonnes	63 m tonnes

Moreover, the strength of the Trade Union Movement meant that industry had to pay much larger amounts in wages and provide for the improvement of conditions in factories and mines. This was long overdue but it happened at a time when most of the big industries were losing money and output was falling. There were many strikes in the 1920s and the unions were mostly successful in preventing business from solving their problems by ordering wage cuts or redundancies.

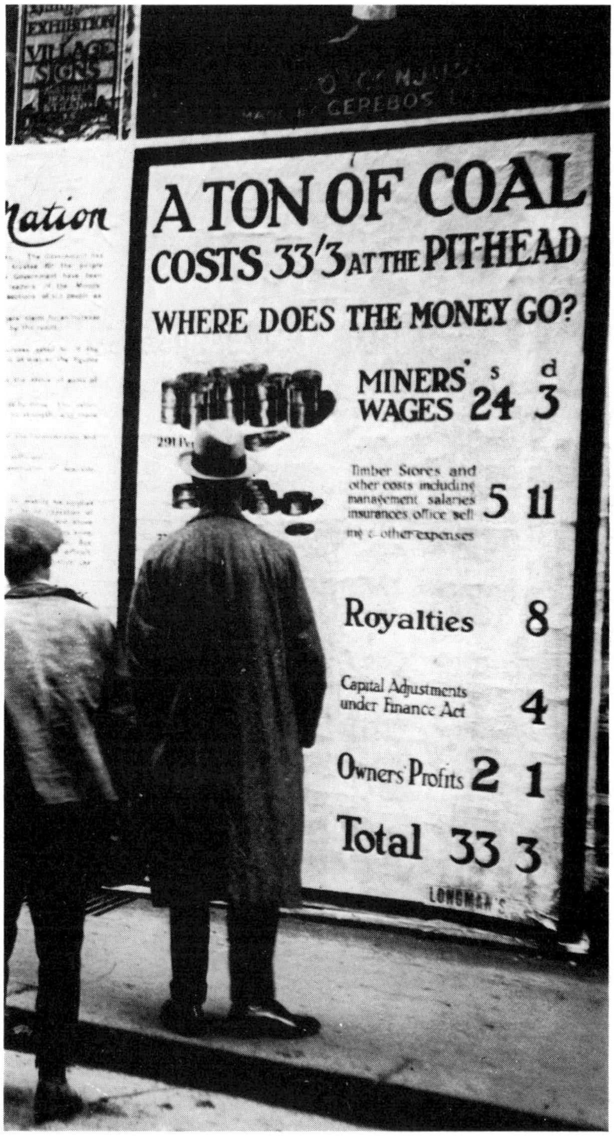

F Coal Profits – a poster from 1926.

?

1. Look at source B. What can you tell about the industrial strength of Britain compared with America in 1900?
2. Look at source D. Who is the richest country in this cartoon? Why?
3. Look at source E. Compare 1907 and 1924. Do these figures support the view that the coal industry was in decline? Explain your answer.

THE USA ON THE WORLD STAGE

Throughout the nineteenth and the early part of the twentieth centuries, the USA had tended to ignore what was going on in Europe. They believed in isolationism – keeping well away from events in Europe that might drag them into war. Towards the end of the last century they had decided to use their growing industrial power to take a stronger and more forceful part in world affairs. In 1900 the president said:

G We must not shrink from playing our part among great nations . . . our history has been one of expansion . . . this is a matter of pride.

President William McKinley

An American Empire

H Uncle Sam builds his empire.

At the end of the nineteenth century President McKinley had taken America to war with Spain and the Americans had begun to build an American Empire out of lands previously held by Spain and Mexico. America had also bought some French and British possessions and had begun to emerge out of isolation.

In wars with Mexico and Spain, America took territories like the Philippines, Puerto Rico, and Guam. It also began to build a navy big enough to protect its new lands and its expanding trade in the Pacific.

Theodore Roosevelt (President from 1901 to 1908) had predicted:

I Our place must be great among nations.

President Theodore Roosevelt

In 1919 America emerged from the war as the most powerful nation on earth – a position shown by Wilson's leading role in the Peace Conference at Versailles. At this conference Wilson was seen by many as the most dominant personality – as this cartoon, dating from the time of Versailles, shows:

J Wilson taking the scissors to old Europe.

Wilson seemed about to prove that America was the most important power in the world by leading the nations at Versailles into a new era. As it happened, his own Senate disagreed with him and the Americans voted to return to isolationism. But things were never to be the same again. Even with America withdrawn into its shell for a while, the Europeans recognised its new importance, as source K shows.

THE GAP IN THE BRIDGE.

K The USA fails to bridge the gap.

Mass Society

'Mass Society' is the name given to the consumer and communications boom that followed the end of the First World War. It was partly the result of post-war prosperity in the USA, and partly the result of the scientific advances that had taken place in the war which had peacetime applications. The American economy in the 1920s went into a terrific period of expansion. There was zero inflation, full employment and a ten per cent drop in the price of manufactured goods. All this and the growth of mass production meant that all sorts of new and exciting products were within the range of all American families.

L It was a time when any miracle seemed possible. No-one knew what was going to arrive in the shops next: gramophones, refrigerators, telephones . . . and at night you could go to Edison's Moving Pictures. What in? Your automobile, of course!

Erl Wilkie

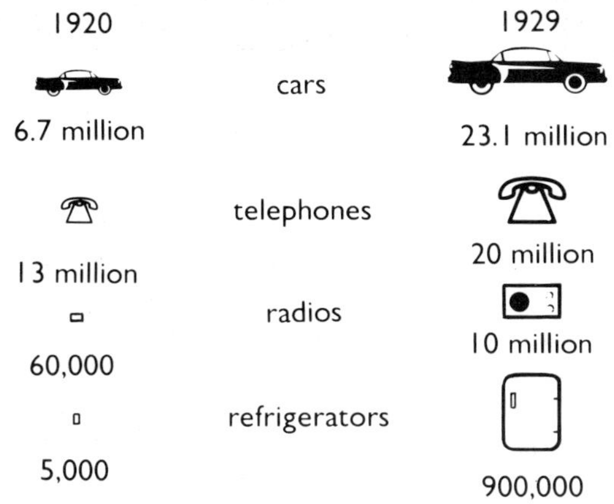

M Consumer boom.

Communications

Some of the technology developed for the First World War was easily adapted for civilian use, like the radio. The electronic revolution helped people to enjoy the new Hollywood films and the new broadcasting stations. Records were mass produced to be played on the new gramophones. Mass production motor cars were followed by a sudden growth in petrol stations, garages and road building. In America, thousands of eating places, diners, were built beside the roads.

Transport-Motor vehicles

N The birth of the traffic jam.

Aeroplanes were bigger, faster and safer. By 1922 British airlines were flying 220,000 kilometres a month and the first Airline companies were set up.

?

1. Use sources G, H, I and K. How consistent was American foreign policy between 1900 and 1919?
2. Look at source J. How accurate is this view of President Wilson at the Peace Conference in 1919?
3. Look at source K. Why is America seen as the keystone of the bridge? Why is the bridge incomplete in the cartoon?
4. According to the text and the sources, what were the beneficial effects of the First World War for society?

INDEX